Take up
CROCHET

Take up
CROCHET

SUE WHITING

MEREHURST

Published in 1994 by
Merehurst Limited
Ferry House, 51-57 Lacy Road,
Putney, London SW15 1PR

ISBN 1 85391 200 X

Edited by Alison Wormleighton
Designed by Kit Johnson
Photography by Di Lewis
Illustrations by Paul Bryant
Charts by King & King

101081694

Typesetting by
Litho Link Limited, Welshpool, Powys

Colour separation by
Fotographics Limited,
UK – Hong Kong

Printed in Italy by
New Interlitho SpA, Milan

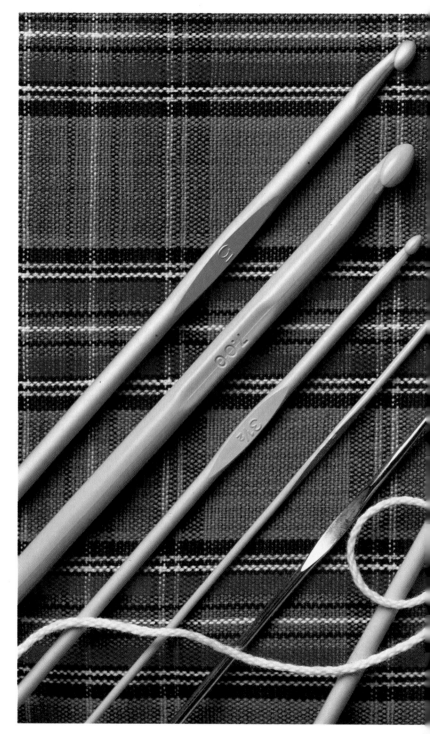

CONTENTS

CROCHET is an immensely absorbing and enjoyable craft, which is easy to learn and quick to work. Because it is based on just a few simple stitches, you can create really attractive items as soon as you have learned the basic techniques. Beautiful textured effects are possible in crochet, from delicate, lacy openwork in fine cotton to bold, colourful designs in chunky wool. This book gives you the chance to try them out for yourself, introducing you to the principal techniques and developing your crochet skills through a variety of inspiring projects.

INTRODUCTION

It's surprisingly easy to learn how to crochet;
you'll soon pick up how to make the various stitches and how
to follow a pattern. You don't need a lot of equipment –
simply a ball of yarn and a crochet hook!

Crochet hooks

Crochet hooks are available in a wide variety of sizes, from very fine metal hooks that are as thin as wire to big chunky plastic ones as thick as a pencil. The size needed is determined by the thickness of the yarn to be used. Every crochet pattern will tell you what size hook you need, and the ball band of the yarn may tell you too.

Crochet hooks fall into three groups. Steel hooks are very fine and are for delicate work with fine crochet cotton. Aluminium hooks are more suited to standard hand-knitting-weight yarns. Plastic hooks are used mainly for thick yarn; as they are not as strong as aluminium ones, they can bend or break.

There are two different methods used to size crochet hooks in Britain – the old-fashioned English imperial sizes, and the European metric system now widely adopted in Britain. The conversion chart opposite shows you how the sizes match up between the two systems and gives you an idea of the thickness of the yarn you would use with each hook size. Although it is important to use the correct size of hook for the yarn, sometimes a much larger or smaller hook will be used to create a special effect.

Yarns for crochet

While any yarn can be used for crochet, some are easier to work with than others. The most important factor is the way the yarn is constructed. It needs to be smooth and firmly twisted so that you don't split it when inserting the hook or pulling a loop through.

Probably the best known type is **crochet cotton** designed specifically for crochet. Ideal for lacy edgings and mats, cushion covers, tablecloths and filet crochet, it comes in a variety of thicknesses and is 'sized' – the higher the number, the finer the yarn. Made of pure cotton, crochet cotton is therefore smooth and is often what is called a perlé yarn. This has a definite cabled appearance where you can see how the strands are twisted together. Also, it does not unravel easily. The main disadvantage for the beginner is that, even in its thickest form, it is still very fine – so whatever you decide to make with it will be made using a fine steel hook and will have to be small if you are to complete it soon.

It is, however, possible to find hand-knitting yarns with a perlé construction that are much thicker and therefore easier to work with and more suited to large items. These are frequently made of light, synthetic fibres, such as acrylic.

Crêpe yarns are also good for crochet as they are usually smooth and their construction holds together the strands making up the yarn. **Standard hand-knitting** yarns, such as pure wool or wool/acrylic mix double knitting, are suitable for crochet too.

Crochet patterns

Crochet patterns are written in a similar way to hand-knitting patterns. Many of the words have standard abbreviations to save space. The list opposite gives the standard abbreviations used for the patterns in this book. Any special terms that relate to the specific pattern are given with that pattern.

STEEL HOOKS

METRIC (mm)	IMPERIAL	APPROXIMATE SUITABLE YARN WEIGHT
0.60	6	crochet cotton
0.75	5	
1.00	4	
1.25	3	
1.50	2½	
1.75	2	

ALUMINIUM OR PLASTIC HOOKS

METRIC (mm)	IMPERIAL	APPROXIMATE SUITABLE YARN WEIGHT
2.00	14	crochet cotton
2.25	13	
2.50	12	
3.00	11	4-ply
3.25	10	
3.50	9	double knitting
3.75	–	
4.00	8	
4.50	7	Aran
5.00	6	
5.50	5	chunky
6.00	4	
6.50	3	
7.00	2	double chunky
8.00	0	
9.00	00	
10.00	000	

STANDARD ABBREVIATIONS

beg	beginning	**patt**	pattern
ch	chain	**rep**	repeat
cont	continue	**RS**	right side
dc	double crochet	**sp (s)**	space(s)
dec	decreas(e) (ing)	**ss**	slip stitch
dtr	double treble	**st (s)**	stitch(es)
foll	following	**tr**	treble
htr	half treble	**WS**	wrong side
inc	increas(e) (ing)	**yo**	yarn over hook

Other equipment

Other than your pattern, yarn and crochet hook, you need a tape measure or ruler to measure certain items, especially to check tension. You will need scissors to trim off the ends and a thick, blunt-ended needle to sew the pieces together. An iron will also be needed, as you should press your completed work.

Pressing and blocking

The way a piece of crochet should be pressed depends on the fibre content of the yarn used to make it. Always check the ball band of your yarn to see what recommendations there are. Avoid pressing from the right side, or, if you do, the work should always be covered by a cloth. Never let a bare iron touch your work, and never use steam or a damp cloth with synthetic fibres.

Some types of crocheted items cannot be pressed flat due to their textured surface, or are difficult to press due to the lacy nature of the fabric. These items are best blocked. Start by dampening the work slightly, using a water spray. Now pin the piece out flat onto a soft surface, following the measurements given with the pattern. A piece of chipboard covered with a towel is an ideal surface, as it allows you to push the pins in neatly. If there is a fancy shaped edge, pin out each point to get the correct effect. Once the item has been pinned into position, simply leave it to dry naturally. As the fabric dries it will 'set' itself into position.

THE BASIC STITCHES

Crochet is a series of loops of yarn, or stitches,
arranged to create different effects. There are only three basic
types of crochet stitch: chain stitch, double crochet stitch and
treble. All the others are variations of these.

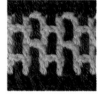

To create the stitches, the crochet hook is used to pull loops of yarn through the loop that is already on the hook, linking the existing loop to ones already made. However, unlike hand knitting, there is only ever one stitch, or loop, left on the hook at the end of each row – which means that you have far less chance of dropping stitches!

The three basic stitches

One of the simplest and most commonly used crochet stitches, **double crochet** stitch is almost the shortest of all the stitches. It is abbreviated **dc**. **Slip stitch** is the simplest and shortest crochet stitch and is sometimes called 'single crochet'. One of the most common uses for it is to join lengths of chain stitches to form the ring that becomes the basis of a circular piece of work. It is also used for shaping but is seldom used on its own. It is abbreviated **ss**. A **treble stitch** is taller than a double crochet stitch. This height is obtained by increasing the number of times one loop of yarn is pulled through two others. Treble stitch is abbreviated **tr**.

These three stitches form the basis of all crochet work and can produce a wide variety of effects. And, as all other crochet stitches are simply variations of these three, once they are mastered you will easily be able to tackle the more complicated stitches.

Getting started

There are set conventions as to exactly how you should hold the hook, the work and the yarn when crocheting; the best way is the way you are happiest with. If you are used to hand knitting, you will probably find it easiest to start by holding the hook and yarn in your right hand – as you do when knitting – and the work in your left hand. When you are more used to making the stitches, you can move on to the 'correct' way shown opposite.

In order to be able to pull loops of new yarn through to form the stitches, you need to start with an initial loop on the hook, as shown opposite.

Once you have the initial loop, or stitch, on your hook, you need to create a 'chain' of more stitches, which will be used to form the foundation of the work. This is called the **foundation chain**.

Each new section of a crochet pattern will start by telling you how many chain stitches to make – the abbreviation used for a chain stitch is **ch**. Once you have your foundation chain, you can start to work crochet stitches into this chain to build up the work.

A pattern will often start by telling you to make, say, ten chain. But, as your initial loop counts as your first chain stitch, you will only actually need to make an extra nine chain. You can count your stitches by counting the number of chain links there are along its length. From one side, the chain looks just like embroidery chain stitch. This chain effect will always appear across the top of the last row of stitches you have worked. When working into the foundation chain, insert the hook through the centre of the chain 'link' but, when working across other stitches, insert the hook under both the loops forming the chain effect.

SLIP LOOP

HOLDING THE YARN AND HOOK

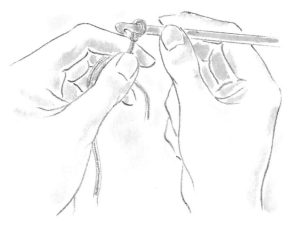

♦ Make a slip loop and pull it up fairly tightly around the neck of the crochet hook. This is your first stitch. All the following stitches that go to make up the finished work will be made from this one stitch.

♦ Hold the hook in your right hand, and the work just below the loop on the hook between the finger and thumb of your left hand. The yarn should be around your left hand so that it is held at an even tension. If you hold it too tightly, you will have problems pulling loops of yarn through. If you hold it too loosely, the loops will be too big.

CHAIN STITCH

1 ♦ Take the yarn from the ball and wind it over and round the hook, from the back to the front.

2 ♦ Pull this new loop of yarn through the loop on the crochet hook. You have made your first chain stitch!

3 ♦ Continue in this way until you have made the required number of stitches.

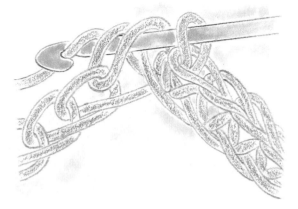

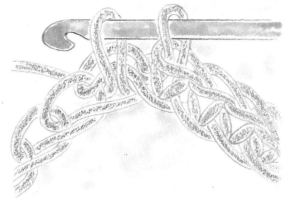

1 ◆ Start by inserting the hook through the work, from the front to the back, under two of the three strands of one of the foundation chain. Take the yarn over and round the hook exactly as for a chain stitch.

2 ◆ Pull the new loop of yarn through the work – you now have two loops on the hook. Take the yarn over and round the hook again in the same way as before.

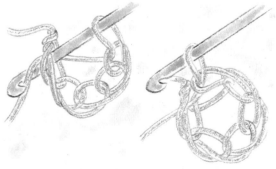

3 ◆ Pull this loop through both the loops on the hook – and you have completed your first double crochet stitch.

◆ A slip stitch is a variation of a double crochet stitch, but you omit the second stage. Start by inserting the hook through the work and take the yarn over the hook exactly as for a double crochet. Now pull this loop of yarn through both the work *and* the loop on the hook. This forms a slip stitch.

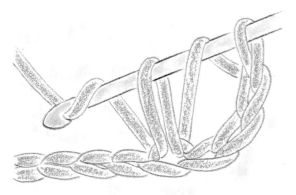

1 ◆ Before inserting the hook through the work, take the yarn over and round the hook in the usual way.

2 ◆ Insert the hook, take the yarn over and round again and pull this loop through the work. Now take the yarn over and round the hook again so that there are four loops on the hook.

3 ◆ Pull this fourth loop of yarn through the second and third loops on the hook, leaving just two loops. Now take the yarn over and round the hook again.

4 ◆ Pull this loop through both loops on the hook. This completes one treble.

CHAIN GANG

The stunning tartan effect of these cushions and throw is simply created by working a basic mesh using just chain and treble stitches, then weaving in and out more lengths of chain.

SIZE

Each cushion measures 40cm (15¾ in) square. The throw measures 140cm (55in) × 153cm (60in).

YOU WILL NEED

Each cushion

50g (2oz) balls of Patons DK in main colour (M):
Red cushion: 4 balls of Diploma Gold in red
Green cushion: 3 balls of Beehive Tumble Dry in green

1 × 50g (2oz) ball of same yarn in each of two contrast colours (A – navy or white, and B – gold)

3.50mm crochet hook

Cushion pad approx 40cm (15¾ in) square

Throw

24 × 50g (2oz) balls of Patons Diploma Gold DK in main colour (M – red)

6 × 50g (2oz) balls of same yarn in each of two contrast colours (A – navy and B – gold)

3.50mm crochet hook

ABBREVIATIONS

See page 9.

TENSION

21 sts and 10 rows to 10cm (4in) measured over basic mesh *before* weaving using 3.50mm hook. 20 sts and 11 rows to 10cm (4in) measured over mesh when woven.

CUSHION WITH SQUARE

For red version of this cushion, use navy for A and gold for B. For green version of this cushion, use white for A and gold for B.
Main Section (Front and Back alike)
Using 3.50mm hook and M, make 84 ch.
Foundation row: 1 tr into 6th ch from hook, *1 ch, miss 1 ch, 1 tr into next ch, rep from * to end, turn. 81 sts. 40 sps.
Now work in mesh patt thus:
1st row: 3 ch (counts as first tr), *1 ch, miss 1 ch, 1 tr into next tr, rep from * to end working last tr into top of turning ch, turn.
This row forms mesh patt and is repeated.
Keeping mesh patt correct, now work a further 42 rows in following stripe sequence:
4 rows using M, 4 rows using B, 4

rows using M, 2 rows using A, 12 rows using M, 2 rows using A, 4 rows using M, 4 rows using B, and 6 rows using M.
Fasten off.
Make second section in exactly the same way.

Weaving
Make 40 lengths of ch approx 44cm (17in) long – make 28 using M, 4 using A and 8 using B.
Attaching ends of ch securely to foundation ch and last row, weave chains in and out of mesh sps, using M for first 4 sps, B for next 4 sps, M for next 4 sps, A for next 2 sps, M for next 12 sps, A for next 2 sps, M for next 4 sps, B for next 4 sps, and M for last 4 sps.

Completing
Join front and back sections along 3 sides. Insert cushion pad and close remaining edge.

CUSHION WITH CROSS
For red version of this cushion, use white for A and gold for B. For green version of this cushion, use navy for A and gold for B.

Main Section
Work exactly as for Cushion with Square but in foll stripe sequence: 13 rows using M, 2 rows using A, 4 rows using M, 4 rows using B, 4 rows using M, 2 rows using A, and 14 rows using M.

Weaving
Make 40 lengths of ch approx 44cm (17in) long – make 32 using M, 4 using A and 4 using B.
Attaching ends of ch securely to foundation ch and last row, weave chains in and out of mesh sps, using M for first 12 sps, A for next 2 sps, M for next 4 sps, B for next 4 sps, M for next 4 sps, A for next 2 sps, and M for last 12 sps.

Completing
Work as for Cushion with Square.

THROW
Using 3.50mm hook and M, make 284 ch.
Work foundation row as for Cushion with Square. 281 sts. 140 sps.
Using M, work a further 5 rows in mesh patt as for Cushion with Square.
Now work a further 162 rows in following stripe sequence: (2 rows using A, 4 rows using M, 4 rows using B, 4 rows using M, 2 rows using A and 12 rows using M) 5 times, 2 rows using A, 4 rows using M, 4 rows using B, 4 rows using M, 2 rows using A and 6 rows using M.
Fasten off.

Weaving
Make 140 lengths of ch approx 168cm (66in) long – make 100 using M, 20 using A and 20 using B.
Attaching ends of ch securely to foundation ch and last row, weave chains in and out of mesh sps, (using M for next 6 sps, A for next 2 sps, M for next 4 sps, B for next 4 sps, M for next 4 sps, A for next 2 sps, and M for next 6 sps) 6 times.

Fringe
Matching colour of yarn to colour of woven ch, cut groups of 3 lengths of yarn approx 25cm (10in) long and knot to foundation ch or final row at end of woven chain. Trim ends even.

MAKING A FABRIC

*Crochet can be worked either in rows, to form a flat
piece of fabric, or in rounds, to form a tube or circle. It is essential
that the stitches are worked at the correct tension.*

Working in rows

When you are crocheting, you are basically working across the top of the new row, and the height of the row is determined by the height of the stitches you use. Work into the top of the previous stitches by inserting the hook through the work, from front to back, under both of the loops forming the chain effect. In order to get to the top of this new row, you will often need to make a short chain at the beginning of a row. This chain is called the **turning chain**. It is made when you turn the work to start the new row, and its length is proportionate to the type of stitch being worked. Each pattern will tell you how many chain stitches to make at the beginning of a row. Sometimes the turning chain is used to form the first stitch of a row; in these cases the pattern will tell you what this chain counts as.

TURNING CHAINS

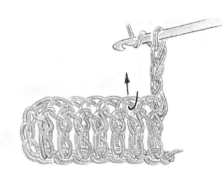

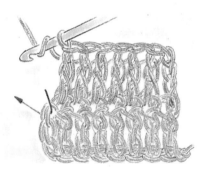

◆ If the turning chain counts as the first stitch of the row, you must work the second stitch into the next stitch of the previous row, missing the stitch at the base of the turning chain. If the turning chain does *not* count as a stitch, then the first stitch of this row must be worked into the stitch which is at the base of the turning chain.

◆ In the same way, if the turning chain formed the first stitch of the previous row, it must be used for the last stitch of the next row. And, obviously, if it does not count as a stitch, do not work into it at the end of a row. Sometimes a pattern will tell you whether you are supposed to work the last stitch of a row into the turning chain. If it does not say, look at your pattern and see what it says the turning chain counts as.

Sometimes the turning chain is in addition to the stitches of the row, and here the pattern will tell you that the chain does not count as a stitch.

Remember when working in rows that, unless you are increasing or decreasing, you *must* have the same number of stitches in each row. It is very easy to turn before the end of a row, or work into the wrong place at the beginning – and create your own shaping!

Shaping

In some crocheted items stitches are increased at certain points to give the required shape. At other times you will need to 'lose' stitches.

A **single increase** of one stitch can be made by simply working twice into the same base stitch. This can be done at any point in the row. Follow the pattern carefully to make sure you work the increase at the right point. This is especially important at the beginning of a row where the turning chain does count as a stitch – you must remember that the increased stitch will be worked into the base of this turning chain, thereby making two stitches. This

method of increasing can also be used to increase more than one stitch – but you will not always achieve the correct effect by working a large number of increased stitches in this way.

Multiple increases can be made at the beginning of a row as if starting a new piece, by making a new foundation chain for these increased stitches. The pattern will tell you to make the required number of new chain stitches – remember that some of these chain stitches will form the foundation chain, and some will form the turning chain.

To **decrease a single stitch** you can simply 'miss' this stitch, in the same way as you missed the first stitch of a row when the turning chain counts as this stitch. This method of decreasing can be used to decrease more than one stitch, but unsightly holes could be formed in the work, especially when the turning chain counts as the first stitch.

To **decrease by working stitches together** is a much better way of decreasing a stitch without forming a hole. When you make any crochet stitch, you are forming a new loop of yarn around the hook

<table>
<tr><td style="text-align:center">**SINGLE INCREASES**</td><td style="text-align:center">**SINGLE DECREASES**</td></tr>
</table>

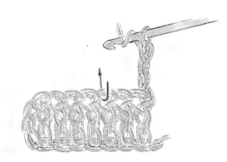

♦ To increase one stitch at the beginning of a row, as shown here, work the correct number of turning chain to count as the first stitch. Then miss the first stitch in the row below and work two stitches into the top of the next stitch. To add a stitch at the end of a row, work two stitches into the top of the last stitch in the row below and then make the last stitch in the usual way into the top of the turning chain.

♦ To decrease one stitch at the beginning of a row, as shown in the diagram here, miss one stitch and work into the next stitch. To decrease one stitch at the end of a row, miss the next to the last stitch and work into the last stitch.

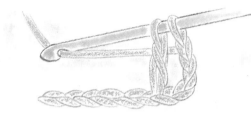

1 ◆ To work two treble stitches together (abbreviated tr2tog) start by working the first treble into the first stitch until there are two loops left on the hook.

2 ◆ Work the second treble into the next stitch, again omitting the last stage. You now have three loops on the hook. Take the yarn over the hook again and pull this loop through all three loops on the hook.

WORKING THREE TREBLES TOGETHER

MULTIPLE DECREASES AT BEGINNING OF ROW

◆ Here, three treble stitches have been worked together. Although the 'legs' are in three different stitches of the previous row, there is only one chain link at the top of the new row where these three stitches are joined.

◆ When working a multiple decrease at the beginning of a row, the slip stitch is useful – simply work slip stitches into each of the stitches to be decreased and, when you have reached the starting point for the new row, work the required turning chain.

and pulling this new loop through two others already on the hook until there is only one loop left on the hook. To work two stitches together, you simply omit the last stage of the first stitch. This method of decreasing stitches by working them together can be used for almost any crochet stitch, and the number of stitches decreased can be quite large. Sometimes, when it is used for effect only, the stitches will not necessarily all be worked into consecutive stitches of a row. The abbreviations section of a pattern will give

full details of how these stitches should be placed and the decrease worked.

Multiple decreases at the end of a row are very easy. You simply miss the required number of stitches at the end of the row and turn the work.

Multiple decreases at the beginning of a row are not quite as simple. To get to the point where this new row will begin, you need to work along the row, over the decreased stitches, at the same level as the previous row.

Working in rounds

One great advantage of crochet is that it is really easy to work a tube or circle of fabric, thus avoiding the need for seams. When working in rounds, the same rules apply as for a fabric made up of rows, except that each round will be joined to the beginning of itself in some way.

As, obviously, the outside edge of a circle is much larger than the centre, when you are working a circular piece of crochet each round will have more stitches in it than the previous one. The way these increases will be worked is exactly the same as if you were working in rows. When working a tubular piece of crochet, each new round will have the same number of stitches as the previous round.

Getting the size right

At the beginning of each pattern you will find a section which is headed Tension. This relates to the number of stitches and rows you need to have within a certain measurement to make your finished item the size of the one in the photograph.

It is vitally important that the tension of your work matches that stated in the pattern. If it does not, you will end up with something the wrong size, and you may either run out of yarn or have a lot left over. In addition, the final fabric will not feel right. If the tension is too tight, the fabric will be stiff and you will find it difficult to work the stitches. If the tension is too loose, the fabric will not hold its shape. Time spent in checking tension is an excellent investment!

JOINING ROUNDS

 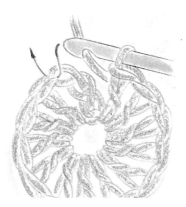 

1 ◆ Most circular pieces of work will start with the ends of the foundation chain being joined, so that you have a ring of stitches. The first round is then often worked, not into the stitches of the chain, but actually into the ring itself. In this case you insert the hook under the whole chain to work the stitch, rather than just through the two loops forming the chain stitch effect.

2 ◆ At the end of a round you will be back at the point where you started. In order to keep the fabric together you need to join the end of the round to the beginning in some way, usually with a slip stitch.

3 ◆ Once the ends are joined, you begin the new round. In the same way as when working in rows, each round will often start with a 'turning chain' to get you to the top of the new round – but, as you rarely turn the work at the beginning of a new round, this is really a starting chain.

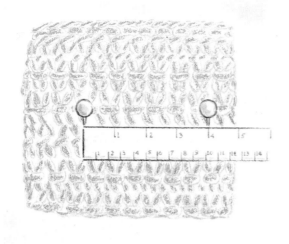

swatch is complete, count out the number of stitches stated, marking the ends with pins.

Measure the distance between the pins – it should measure the same as stated for the tension. If it measures more, you are working too loosely and should change to a finer hook. If it measures less, your work is too tight and you should make another swatch using a larger size of hook. Measure your row tension in exactly the same way and continue to make swatches until you have the tension stated. Whatever size hook you used to get this tension is the size you need to use to make the item.

When working a flat circular piece, the tension is often given as being the diameter of the first few rounds. Once you have made these rounds, measure your work. If this measurement does not match the stated measurement, start again and adjust your hook size as necessary.

◆ *Always make a tension swatch before beginning a crochet pattern.*

If you are working in rows, the tension will tell you how many stitches and rows there should be within a certain measurement – usually 10cm (4in). Before you begin the actual item, make a tension swatch at least 12cm (4¾ in) square. Use the hook and stitch pattern detailed in the tension section and, when the

Fastening off

When you have completed each crochet section, you need to fasten off the yarn before you can begin the next piece. Simply cut off the yarn and thread this end through the loop on the hook. Pull the end up tight and you are ready to start the next section.

First Steps

Worked using just chain and double crochet stitches,
these delicate baby shoes are an ideal way to learn how to
increase and decrease stitches. The shaping is created by working
twice into one stitch for the increases and simply missing
the necessary stitches for the decreases.

SIZE

Finished shoe measures
10cm (4in) from toe to heel.

YOU WILL NEED

1 × 50g (2oz) ball of Coats
Musica 5 crochet cotton

1.75mm crochet hook

1m (1yd) of narrow ribbon

ABBREVIATIONS
See page 9.

TENSION
32 sts and 38 rows to 10cm (4in)
measured over double crochet
fabric using 1.75mm hook.

SHOE (Worked in one piece,
starting at heel edge of sole)
Sole
Using 1.75mm hook, make 7 ch.
1st row (RS): 1 dc into 2nd ch
from hook, 1 dc into each ch to
end, turn. 6 sts.
2nd row: 1 ch (does *not* count as
st), 2 dc into first dc, 1 dc into

each of next 4 dc, 2 dc into last dc,
turn. 8 sts.
3rd row: 1 ch (does *not* count as
st), 2 dc into first dc, 1 dc into
each of next 6 dc, 2 dc into last dc,
turn. 10 sts.
4th row: 1 ch (does *not* count as
st), 1 dc into first dc, 1 dc into
each dc to end, turn.
Last 4 rows set double crochet
fabric, with increased sts at both
ends of 2nd and 3rd row.
Cont as now set, inc one st at
both ends of 7th, 13th and 21st
rows. 16 sts.
Work 12 rows without shaping.
Now dec one st at both ends of
next row. 14 sts.
Work one row.
Dec one st at both ends of next 3
rows. 8 sts.
This completes sole section.
Shape upper
Inc one st at both ends of next 7
rows and foll 4 alt rows. 32 sts.
Shape first side
54th row (WS): 1 ch (does *not*
count as st), 1 dc into first dc, 1 dc
into each of next 8 dc, turn.
Work on these 9 sts only for first
side.

*Dec one st at beg of next row. 8
sts.
Work one row.
Inc one st at end of next row. 9 sts.
Work one row.
Inc one st at beg of next row and
at same edge of foll 2 rows. 12 sts.
Inc one st at both ends of next
row. 14 sts.
Make buttonhole
63rd row: 1 ch (does *not* count as
st), 1 dc into each of first 2 dc, 1
ch, miss 1 dc, 1 dc into each of
next 11 dc, turn.
64th row: 1 ch (does *not* count as
st), 1 dc into each of first 11 dc, 1
dc into next ch sp, 1 dc into each
of last 2 dc, turn.
Work one row.
Inc one st at beg and dec one st at
end of next row. 14 sts.
Work 1 row.
Dec one st at end of next and foll
2 alt rows. 11 sts.
Work 4 rows. Fasten off.*
Shape front tab
Return to last complete row
worked before first side, and miss
first 2 dc after first side, attach
yarn to next st and proceed as
follows:

54th row (WS): 1 ch (does *not* count as st), 1 dc into dc where yarn is attached, 1 dc into each of next 7 dc, turn.

Work on these 8 sts only for front tab.

Dec one st at both ends of next 2 rows. 4 sts.

Work 16 rows. Fasten off.

Shape second side

Return to last complete row worked before first side and front tab, miss first 2 dc after front tab, attach yarn to next st and proceed as follows:

54th row (WS): 1 ch (does *not* count as st), 1 dc into dc where yarn is attached, 1 dc into each of next 8 dc, turn.

Work on these 9 sts only for second side.

Now complete second side as for first side by working from * to *, reversing shaping by working it at opposite end of row to first side and making buttonhole in 63rd and 64th rows thus:

Make buttonhole

63rd row: 1 ch (does *not* count as st), 1 dc into each of first 11 dc, 1 ch, miss 1 dc, 1 dc into each of next 2 dc, turn.

64th row: 1 ch (does *not* count as st), 1 dc into each of first 2 dc, 1 dc into next ch sp, 1 dc into each of last 11 dc, turn.

MAKING UP

Join heel seam of sides. Matching heel seam to centre of foundation chain edge of sole, sew upper to sole. Starting and ending at end of front tab, work one row of dc along entire upper edge of shoe. Fasten off. Fold last 8 rows of front tab to inside and stitch in place. Cut ribbon into 2 equal lengths and thread each length through buttonholes and loop of front tab. Tie the two ends in a bow on top of foot.

GOING IN CIRCLES

This pretty lacy mat worked in rounds has a
scalloped edge made from a combination of trebles
and chains, with the chains doubled back on themselves
to create the fancy edge. The central flower section
uses mainly trebles, and the mesh effect is
achieved by working chain loops.

SIZE

Finished panel is 29cm
(11⅜in) in diameter at its
widest point.

YOU WILL NEED

1 × 50g (2oz) ball of Coats
Opera 5 crochet cotton

1.75mm crochet hook

ABBREVIATIONS
See page 9.

Special abbreviations: tr3tog –
(yo, insert hook into next st and
draw loop through, yo and draw
loop through 2 loops on hook) 3
times, yo, and draw loop through
all 4 loops on hook; **tr4tog** – (yo,
insert hook into next st and draw
loop through, yo and draw loop
through 2 loops on hook) 4 times,
yo, and draw loop through all 5
loops on hook; **tr5tog** – (yo, insert
hook into next st and draw loop
through, yo and draw loop

through 2 loops on hook) 5 times,
yo, and draw loop through all 6
loops on hook.

TENSION
First 4 rounds measure 5cm (2in)
in diameter.

CROCHET PANEL
Using 1.75mm hook, make 8 ch
and join with a ss to form a ring.
Working in rounds, proceed thus:
1st round (RS): 1 ch (does *not*
count as st), 16 dc into ring, ss to
first dc.
2nd round: 5 ch (counts as 1 tr
and 2 ch), (miss 1 dc, 1 tr into next
dc, 2 ch) 7 times, ss to 3rd of 5 ch
at beg of round.
3rd round: 3 ch (counts as 1 tr),
4 tr into next ch sp, (1 tr into next
tr, 4 tr into next ch sp) 7 times, ss
to top of 3 ch at beg of round.
4th round: 3 ch (counts as 1 tr),
1 tr into base of 3 ch, *1 tr into
each of next 3 tr**, 2 tr into each
of next 2 tr, rep from * to end,
ending last rep at **, 2 tr into next
tr, ss to top of 3 ch at beg of
round.

5th round: 3 ch (counts as 1 tr), 1 tr into base of 3 ch, 1 tr into each of next 3 tr, 1 ch, 1 tr into each of next 3 tr, *2 tr into next tr, 1 tr into each of next 3 tr, 1 ch, 1 tr into each of next 3 tr, rep from * to end, ss to top of 3 ch at beg of round.

6th round: ss to next tr, 3 ch (counts as 1 tr), 1 tr into base of 3 ch, 1 tr into each of next 2 tr, 2 ch, miss 1 tr, 1 dc into next ch sp, 2 ch, miss 1 tr, 1 tr into each of next 2 tr, 2 tr into next tr, 1 ch, (2 tr into next tr, 1 tr into each of next 2 tr, 2 ch, miss 1 tr, 1 dc into next ch sp, 2 ch, miss 1 tr, 1 tr into each of next 2 tr, 2 tr into next tr, 1 ch) 7 times, ss to top of 3 ch at beg of round.

7th round: ss to next tr, 3 ch (counts as 1 tr), 1 tr into each of next 2 tr, 1 tr into next ch sp, 1 ch, miss 1 dc, 1 tr into next ch sp, 1 tr into each of next 3 tr, 2 ch, miss 1 tr, 1 dc into next ch sp, 2 ch, miss 1 tr, (1 tr into each of next 3 tr, 1 tr into next ch sp, 1 ch, miss 1 dc, 1 tr into next ch sp, 1 tr into each of next 3 tr, 2 ch, miss 1 tr, 1 dc into next ch sp, 2 ch, miss 1 tr) 7 times, ss to top of 3 ch at beg of round.

8th round: ss to next tr, 3 ch (counts as 1 tr), 1 tr into each of next 2 tr, 1 tr into next ch sp, 1 tr into each of next 3 tr, 2 ch, miss 1 tr, 1 dc into next ch sp, 4 ch, miss 1 dc, 1 dc into next ch sp, 2 ch, miss 1 tr, (1 tr into each of next 3 tr, 1 tr into next ch sp, 1 tr into each of next 3 tr, 2 ch, miss 1 tr, 1 dc into next ch sp, 4 ch, miss 1 dc, 1 dc into next ch sp, 2 ch, miss 1 tr) 7 times, ss to top of 3 ch at beg of round.

9th round: ss to next tr, 3 ch, tr4tog over next 4 tr, *4 ch, miss 1 tr, 1 dc into next ch sp, 4 ch, miss 1 dc, 1 dc into next ch sp, 4 ch, miss 1 dc, 1 dc into ch sp**, 4 ch, miss 1 tr, tr5tog over next 5 tr, rep from * to end, ending last rep at **, 2 ch, miss 1 tr, 1 tr into top of tr4tog at beg of round.

10th round: (5 ch, 1 dc into next ch sp) to end, 4 ch, 1 dc into top of tr at end of previous round.

11th round: 2 ch, tr3tog working first leg around dc at end of previous round and next 2 legs into first ch sp, 5 ch, (tr4tog working 2 legs into ch sps either side of next dc, 5 ch) to end, ss to top of tr3tog.

12th round: 8 ch (counts a 1 tr and 5 ch), (1 tr into next tr4tog, 5 ch) to end, ss to 3rd of 8 ch at beg of round.

13th round: 1 ch (does *not* count as st), 1 dc into base of 1 ch. * (4 ch, 1 dc into next ch sp) twice**, 4 ch, 1 dc into next tr, rep from * to end, ending last rep at **, 2 ch, 1 htr into first dc.

14th round: (5 ch, 1 dc into next ch sp) to end, 2 ch, 1 tr into htr at end of previous round.

15th round: 8 ch (counts as 1 tr and 5 ch), (1 tr into next ch sp, 5 ch) to end, ss to 3rd of 8 ch at beg of round.

Rep 13th to 15th rounds once more.

19th round: ss to centre of first ch sp, 1 ch (does *not* count as st), 1 dc into first ch sp, *5 ch, 1 dc into next ch sp, 3 ch, (1 tr, 1 ch, 1 tr, 1 ch, 1 tr, 1 ch and 1 tr) into next ch sp, 3 ch, 1 dc into next ch sp**, (5 ch, 1 dc into next ch sp) 3 times, rep from * to end, ending last rep at **, (5 ch, 1 dc into next ch sp) twice, 2 ch, 1 tr into first dc.

20th round: 1 ch (does *not* count as st), *1 dc into next ch sp, 5 ch, 1 dc into next ch sp, (2 ch, 1 tr into next ch sp) 5 times, 2 ch**, (1 dc into next ch sp, 5 ch) twice, rep from * to end, ending last rep at **, 1 dc into next ch sp, 5 ch, 1 dc into next ch sp, 2 ch, 1 tr into first dc.

21st round: 1 ch (does *not* count as st), *1 dc into next ch sp, 5 ch, 1 dc into next ch sp, (2 tr into next ch sp, 1 tr into next tr) 5 times, 2 tr into next ch sp, 1 dc into next ch sp**, 5 ch, rep from * to end, ending last rep at **, 2 ch, 1 tr into first dc.

22nd round: *5 ch, 1 dc into next ch sp, 3 ch, miss (1 dc and 1 tr), (1 tr into next tr, 3 ch, ss to top of tr just worked, 2 ch, miss 1 tr) 7 times, 1 tr into next tr, 3 ch, ss to top of tr just worked, 3 ch**, 1 dc into next ch sp, rep from * to end, ending last rep at **, ss to tr at end of last round.
Fasten off.

MAKING UP
Pin the mat out flat and press the crochet panel lightly from the wrong side.

TREBLE STITCH VARIATIONS

A half treble is just slightly taller than a
double crochet and makes a firm, compact fabric, while double
treble and triple treble are very tall and produce a
looser, more open effect.

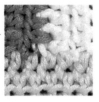

You have already seen how to vary a double crochet to make it shorter to form a slip stitch, or to make it taller to form a treble, and all the other stitches are varied in the same way, since all crochet stitches are variations of the chain, double crochet and treble stitch. Stitches are made shorter by pulling the new loop through more than two existing loops at once, as for the slip stitch. Stitches are made taller by winding the yarn round the hook before it is inserted into the work, as for the treble.

The **double treble** – abbreviated **dtr** – is taller than a treble. Its name comes from the fact that, whereas for a treble the yarn is wrapped round the hook (abbreviated **yo**) once before it is inserted into the work, for a double treble the yarn is wrapped round the hook twice before inserting it.

THE DOUBLE TREBLE

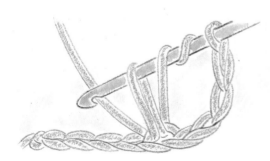

1 ◆ For a double treble, work 'yo' twice and insert the hook into the work. Work another 'yo' and pull this loop through the work – there should now be four loops on the hook.

2 ◆ Work 'yo' and draw this loop through two loops – there are now three loops on the hook. Repeat the 'yo and draw through 2 loops' process until you are left with just one loop on the hook. Your double treble is now complete.

While the double crochet is a short, square stitch, and the treble a tall, thin stitch, the **half treble** is midway between the two. Abbreviated **htr**, it is exactly what its name implies – half a treble stitch.

In the same way as a double treble is bigger than a treble, you can continue to increase the height of the stitch by increasing the number of times the yarn is wrapped around the hook before it is inserted into the work. As its name suggests, the **triple treble**, abbreviated **trtr** or, sometimes, **ttr**, is made by wrapping the yarn round the hook three times.

Similarly, a **quadruple treble**, or **qtr**, has the yarn wound round the hook four times before inserting it. A **quintuple treble**, or **qttr**, has the 'yo' worked five times, a **sextuple treble**, or **str**, has it worked six times, and so on. As the number of times the 'yo' is worked before inserting the hook increases, so the number of times the 'yo and draw through 2 loops' process is repeated.

THE HALF TREBLE

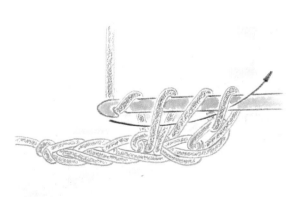

◆ For a half treble, start by working the first stage of a treble. Take the yarn over and round the hook and insert the hook into the work. Pull the loop through so that you have three loops on the hook. For a treble, at this point you would work 'yo' and draw through two loops twice – but for a half treble work 'yo' and draw this loop through all three loops on the hook.

THE TRIPLE TREBLE

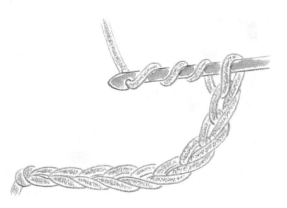

◆ For a triple treble wind the yarn round the hook three times before inserting it into the work. Once the hook has been inserted, work a 'yo' and pull this loop through the work. Now repeat the 'yo and draw through 2 loops' process until, once again, there is only one loop on the hook.

SQUARE ROOTS

*This double-bed-sized bedspread is made of lots of
individual squares worked in half trebles, then joined to
create a classic log-cabin patchwork effect. Even using a thick
cotton yarn, it may take you a while to make – but you'll
end up with an heirloom to treasure!*

SIZE

Finished bedspread
measures approx 240cm
(94in) × 260cm (101in).

YOU WILL NEED

28 × 50g (2oz) balls of
Patons Classic Cotton DK in
main colour (M – white)

27 × 50g (2oz) balls of same
yarn in each of two contrast
colours (A – blue and B –
yellow)

3.50mm crochet hook

ABBREVIATIONS
See page 9.

TENSION
Each motif measures 20.5cm (8in)
square using 3.50mm hook.

BASIC MOTIF
Using 3.50mm hook and first
colour, make 10 ch.
1st row: 1 htr into 3rd ch from
hook, 1 htr into each of next 7 ch,
turn. 9 sts.

2nd row: 2 ch (counts as first st),
1 htr into each of next 8 sts, turn.
Rep 2nd row 4 times more.
Change to second colour.
7th row: 2 ch (counts as first st), 1
htr into each of next 7 sts, 3 htr
into next st, now work 8 htr evenly
along adjacent row end edge,
turn.
8th row: 2 ch (counts as first st), 1
htr into each of next 8 sts, 3 htr
into next st, 1 htr into each of next
9 sts, turn.
9th row: 2 ch (counts as first st), 1
htr into each of next 9 sts, 3 htr
into next st, 1 htr into each of next
10 sts, turn.
10th row: 2 ch (counts as first st),
1 htr into each of next 10 sts, 3 htr
into next st, 1 htr into each of next
11 sts, do not turn.
Change to third colour.
11th row: 2 ch (counts as first st),
11 htr along adjacent row end
edge, 3 htr into corner, 12 htr
along next edge, turn.
12th row: 2 ch (counts as first st),
1 htr into each of next 12 sts, 3 htr
into next st, 1 htr into each of next
13 sts, turn.
13th row: 2 ch (counts as first st),
1 htr into each of next 13 sts, 3 htr

into next st, 1 htr into each of
next 14 sts, turn.
14th row: 2 ch (counts as first st),
1 htr into each of next 14 sts, 3 htr
into next st, 1 htr into each of next
15 sts, do not turn.
Change to second colour.
15th row: 2 ch (counts as first st),
4 htr into row end edge of section
just worked using third colour, 1
htr into each of next 11 sts of
previous section worked in
second colour, 3 htr into next
(corner) st, 1 htr into each of next
12 sts, 4 htr along row end of
section worked in third colour,
turn.
16th row: 2 ch (counts as first st),
1 htr into each of next 16 sts, 3 htr
into next st, 1 htr into each of next
17 sts, turn.
17th row: 2 ch (counts as first st),
1 htr into each of next 17 sts, 3 htr
into next st, 1 htr into each of next
18 sts, turn.
18th row: 2 ch (counts as first st),
1 htr into each of next 18 sts, 3 htr
into next st, 1 htr into each of next
19 sts, do not turn.
Change to first colour.
19th row: 2 ch (counts as first st),
4 htr into row end edge of section

just worked using second colour, 1 htr into each of next 15 sts of previous section worked in third colour, 3 htr into next (corner) st,

1 htr into each of next 16 sts, 4 htr along row end of section worked in second colour, turn.

20th row: 2 ch (counts as first st),

1 htr into each of next 20 sts, 3 htr into next st, 1 htr into each of next 21 sts, turn.

21st row: 2 ch (counts as first st), 1 htr into each of next 21 sts, 3 htr into next st, 1 htr into each of next 22 sts, turn.

22nd row: 2 ch (counts as first st), 1 htr into each of next 22 sts, 3 htr into next st, 1 htr into each of next 23 sts, do not turn.
Change to second colour.

23rd row: 2 ch (counts as first st), 4 htr into row end edge of section just worked using first colour, 1 htr into each of next 19 sts of previous section worked in second colour, 3 htr into next (corner) st, 1 htr into each of next 20 sts, 4 htr along row end of section worked in first colour, turn.

24th row: 2 ch (counts as first st), 1 htr into each of next 24 sts, 3 htr into next st, 1 htr into each of next 25 sts, turn.

25th row: 2 ch (counts as first st), 1 htr into each of next 25 sts, 3 htr into next st, 1 htr into each of next 26 sts, turn.

26th row: 2 ch (counts as first st), 1 htr into each of next 26 sts, 3 htr into next st, 1 htr into each of next 27 sts, do not turn.
Change to third colour.

27th row: 2 ch (counts as first st), 4 htr into row end edge of section just worked using second colour, 1 htr into each of next 23 sts of previous section worked in first colour, 3 htr into next (corner) st, 1 htr into each of next 24 sts, 4 htr along row end of section worked in second colour, turn.

28th row: 2 ch (counts as first st), 1 htr into each of next 28 sts, 3 htr

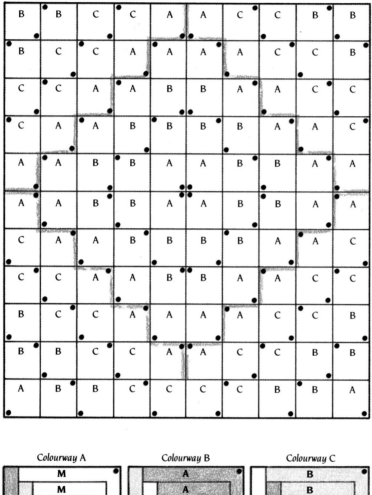

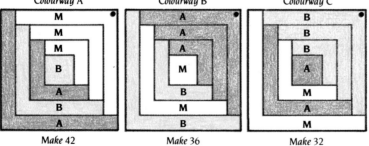

Colourway A   Colourway B   Colourway C

Make 42   Make 36   Make 32

KEY   M *white*   A *blue*   B *yellow*

into next st, 1 htr into each of next 29 sts, turn.

29th row: 2 ch (counts as first st), 1 htr into each of next 29 sts, 3 htr into next st, 1 htr into each of next 30 sts, turn.

30th row: 2 ch (counts as first st), 1 htr into each of next 30 sts, 3 htr into next st, 1 htr into each of next 31 sts.

Fasten off.

Motif is a square, divided diagonally – one half is solid colour and other striped. On diagrams, a dot marks solid-coloured corner.

BEDSPREAD
Main Section

Following diagrams opposite, make 110 motifs in total – 42 in colourway A, 36 in colourway B, and 32 in colourway C. Join motifs to form one large rectangle which is 10 motifs wide by 11 motifs long. To join motifs, hold them RS facing and work 1 dc through edge sts of motifs. Work around shapes, joining like-coloured edges so that seam is invisible – see blue line on diagram on opposite page.

Edging

Rejoin M to outer edge of Main Section with RS facing and proceed as follows:

1st round (RS): 2 ch (counts as first st), work 1 htr into each st to end, working 3 htr into corner sts as before, ss to top of 2 ch, turn. Rep this round 3 times more using M.

Break off M, join in A and work a further 3 rounds.

Break off A, join in B and work a further 3 rounds.

Fasten off.

MAKING
AND JOINING MOTIFS

One of the classic forms of crochet work is that
made up of motifs, in which lots of small, identical pieces of
crochet – the motifs – are joined to form one large item.

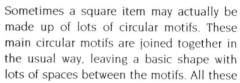

Motif work has many advantages. One great bonus is that you are only ever working one small piece, thereby avoiding the need to carry around large sections – ideal when travelling! Also, as you will make a lot of the same motif, you quickly learn what you are doing.

Whatever shape a motif is, it is usually worked in rounds. The specific shaping needed to create the final design will be fully explained in the pattern.

Even square motifs can start with a circle – the angles are formed by working more and longer stitches at the four corner points. These stitches can be taller stitches than those used along the sides, or simply more chain stitches if it is a lacy motif.

Joining motifs
Motifs can be joined together to make up the finished item in a variety of different ways. Some are joined as they are worked, while others are sewn together afterwards. If the way the motifs are to be joined is very simple, a pattern may simply tell you to join the motifs to form a square or rectangle with a certain number of motifs in each of the rows. Although a pattern may tell you one way to join motifs, you may find it easier to join them in another way.

Even if a pattern says to join the motifs as you work, you may prefer to make them all separately and hand sew them together afterwards. There is no reason why you should not – but remember to fasten off the threads securely.

Sometimes a square item may actually be made up of lots of circular motifs. These main circular motifs are joined together in the usual way, leaving a basic shape with lots of spaces between the motifs. All these spaces are then filled with smaller, filling motifs. These filling motifs can be made in a similar way to the main motifs and joined during their last round, using the same method as for the main motifs.

Sometimes the filling motifs do not start with a basic chain loop in the same way as the main motifs, but are worked straight into the loops, or stitches, of the main motifs. Take care to read the pattern to find out exactly where you are to start, and make sure you work them from the correct side!

Adapting items
Once you have got the hang of how to make and join the motifs there is no reason why you have to make the actual item shown. You can play around and join the motifs together to form any size or shape you want. If you particularly like a motif which is used to make a tablecloth, for example, but you think that it may be too much for you to finish, you can make fewer motifs and use the resulting shape as a cushion cover, a table mat or a tray cloth. Similarly, if a motif is shown used as a tablecloth and you want a bedspread, simply keep making and joining more motifs until it is the size you want, planning out how the motifs will be joined yourself.

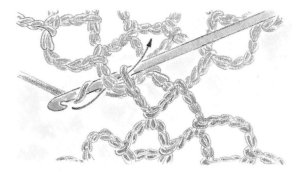

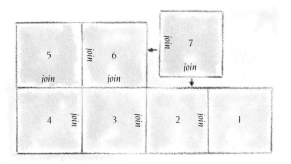

◆ If a motif has a lot of loops of chain stitches around the edge, it is easy to join these motifs as they are made. Complete the first motif, which is the one the others will eventually be joined to. Now make another, stopping before the last round. Holding the first motif against this one with the wrong sides together, start to work this last round. Join the motifs at the points specified in the pattern by using a slip stitch, or double crochet, to replace the central chain stitch of each loop where a join occurs, working it around the corresponding chain loop on the first motif.

◆ It is easiest to join motifs into rows, and then to work another row of motifs, joining this row to the first row as you go. If the motifs are square, they will be joined to each other along opposite sides only for the first row. The first motif of the second row will then be joined to one end motif along the side adjacent to the edge already joined. For all the other motifs of this row, they will be joined along two adjacent edges – to the last motif made and to the edge of the same motif on the row below.

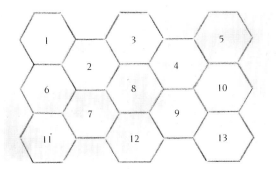

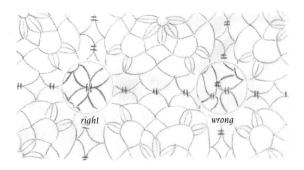

◆ If the way motifs are joined is complicated, a diagram may show you how they are positioned. Work out beforehand the best way to join them, and lightly write in the order you are going to make the motifs on the diagram. Alternatively, simply mark on the diagram which motifs you have already joined.

◆ When you are joining motifs together at a point where two motifs are already joined, make sure you do this correctly to prevent unwanted holes from forming. This join should be worked *around* the previous join, not next to it.

PERFECT SQUARE

This elegant tablecloth is made up of lots of square lacy motifs joined as you go along. Here the tablecloth is nearly a metre (yard) square, but you could make anything from a small mat of just four motifs to a magnificent bedspread!

SIZE

Finished cloth measures approx 98cm (38½in) square.

YOU WILL NEED

11 × 50g (2oz) balls of Coats Opera 5 crochet cotton (one ball will make approx 17 motifs)

1.75mm crochet hook

ABBREVIATIONS

See page 9.

Special abbreviations: tr2tog – (yo, insert hook into next st and draw loop through, yo and draw loop through 2 loops on hook) twice, yo, and draw loop through all 3 loops on hook; **tr3tog** – (yo, insert hook into next st and draw loop through, yo and draw loop through 2 loops on hook) 3 times, yo, and draw loop through all 4 loops on hook.

TENSION

Each motif measures 7cm (2¾in) square using 1.75mm hook.

BASIC MOTIF

Using 1.75mm hook, make 8 ch and join with ss to form a ring.

1st round: 1 ch (does *not* count as st), 16 dc into ring, ss to first dc.

2nd round: 3 ch, tr2tog into dc at base of 3 ch (counts as first tr3tog), (3 ch, miss 1 dc, tr3tog into next st) 7 times, 3 ch, miss 1 dc, ss to top of tr2tog at beg of round.

3rd round: 1 ch (does *not* count as st), 1 dc into st at base of 1 ch, (7 ch, miss 3 ch, 1 dc into next tr3tog) 7 times, 3 ch, miss 3 ch, 1 dtr into first dc.

4th round: 3 ch (counts as first tr), 4 tr into sp created by dtr of previous round, *4 ch, 1 dc into next ch sp, 4 ch, (5 tr, 5 ch and 5 tr) into next ch sp, rep from * twice more, 4 ch, 1 dc into next ch sp, 4 ch, 5 tr into next ch sp – same sp as (first 3 ch and 4 tr), 5 ch, ss to top of 3 ch at beg of round.

5th round: 7 ch (counts as 1 tr and 4 ch), *1 dc into next ch sp, 5 ch, 1 dc into next ch sp, 4 ch, (5 tr, 3 ch and 5 tr) into next ch sp, 4 ch, rep from * twice more, 1 dc into next ch sp, 5 ch, 1 dc into next ch sp, 4 ch, (5 tr, 3 ch and 4 tr) into next ch sp, ss to 3rd of 7 ch at beg of round.

Fasten off.

Motif forms a square. In each corner there is a 3 ch sp between 2 groups of 5 tr, and midway along each side there is a 5 ch sp.

TABLECLOTH

Make 196 motifs in all as for Basic Motif, joining them to form a square of 14 rows of 14 motifs. Join motifs while working 5th round by replacing (3 ch) at corners with (1 ch, 1 dc into corner sp of adjacent motif, 1 ch) and along sides by replacing (5 ch) with (2 ch, 1 dc into corresponding sp along side of adjacent motif, 2 ch).

Pin out to measurement given and press.

CROCHET EDGINGS

Once the main crochet section has been made, an
edging is often added to finish off the item. The way this is done
can transform the work – if the edging is wrong, a beautiful
piece of crochet can be ruined!

Attaching the yarn

Often you will need to rejoin the yarn to the work before the edging can be made. To attach the yarn to the point specified in the pattern, start by making a slip loop in the usual way. Slip this over the hook and insert the hook through the work. Take the yarn over and round the hook and pull this loop through both the work and the slip loop. You are now ready to start the edging.

Working the stitches

Crochet edgings are usually made by working directly into the stitches along the edges of the main section. Where you are working across the top of a row, place the stitches under both of the chain-effect loops in the usual way. Across the foundation-chain edge, work through the remaining loop of the chain left at the bottom of each stitch.

The way the stitches are placed along row ends will depend on the stitch used for the main section. If it is a lacy pattern, you may have to work around the chains or trebles along the edges, but if it is a solid double crochet fabric, you may be able to insert the hook through the actual stitches. For some stitch patterns you may need to use a combination of both methods.

Along shaped edges the shaping often creates a stepped effect, and here you will have a combination of row ends and row tops to work into, so use a variety of ways of inserting the hook through the work. If the edging is worked correctly, it will smooth out the edge.

Edgings are often added to pieces to gently pull in and hold what is otherwise rather a loose edge, particularly along the foundation chain edge, where there is a tendency for the work to flute out. It is therefore important that the number of stitches worked for the edging is correct. Even if a pattern specifies the number of stitches to be worked along an edge, you may need to work slightly more or less because of the tension of your work. Or you could work the number stated, using a size smaller hook.

For a very simple edging, a pattern may often just say 'work one row (or round) of double crochet', leaving you to work out exactly how many stitches you should make. If you make too many, the edge will be fluted, but too few will make it pull. The number of stitches you need depends on how loosely you crochet, the type of edge and the type of yarn. As one or two rows of crochet can be very elastic, you need far fewer stitches than you think.

Across the top and bottom of the work, it is probably best to work one stitch for every stitch of the original edge, though you may need to miss a few stitches here and there to keep the edge neat.

The number of stitches you will need along a row-end edge depends on the height of the stitches. As a rough guide, work one stitch for every double crochet row end, and two stitches for every treble row end. Try to keep the number of stitches you work for each type of row-end even so the edge will be smooth.

Many edgings will involve working around a corner. Obviously, you will need more stitches at the corner points so the work will lie flat. Edging stitches are worked into row ends or stitches – and, at the true corner point of a piece, there is neither of these! The point chosen for the corner point of an edging can be the last row end point or the first stitch of the row. The corner point may be specified on your pattern.

If the edging is worked in double crochet, three stitches worked into the corner point will give a neat, slightly rounded, but basically square, corner. The corner point of the next row, or round, of the edging will be the central stitch of this group of three. Every row, or round, will need the three corner stitches.

If you are using taller stitches for the edging, the outer edge will obviously be longer, and so you will need to work more stitches into the corner point. Similarly, if it is not a right-angled corner, you will not need as many stitches.

Lacy and fancy edgings

Not all edgings are as simple as a row or two of one type of stitch – some are lacy patterns themselves. Frequently a pattern will tell you to work a multiple of stitches plus a set amount along an edge for the first row, or round. This is then used as the 'foundation chain' for the patterned edging, and the pattern will not work out correctly if you do not work the correct number, or multiple, of stitches. For a fancy edging, the pattern will usually tell you exactly what stitches to make into the corner point.

The frequently used edging known as **crabstitch** gives a corded appearance. Although it looks complicated, and may take you a while to get the hang of, it is incredibly simple. Crab stitch is simply a row of double crochet worked backwards.

Many edgings use a **picot** to form a little loop that juts out beyond the edge. Picots can be worked on a smooth double crochet edge or as part of a fancy lacy edging. A picot is simply a loop of chain stitches where the ends are joined. The number of chain stitches in a picot, and the way the loop is closed, can vary from pattern to pattern.

The most standard picot is one made up of three or four chain stitches and a slip stitch. At the point where the picot is to be made, work the chain stitches. Now close the loop by working a slip stitch into the first chain stitch of the picot.

CRAB STITCH

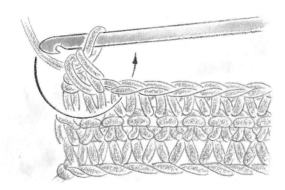

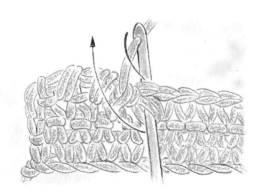

1 ◆ When working in rows of double crochet, the work is turned at the beginning of each row in order to start the next. For crab stitch do not turn your work, but insert the hook into the last stitch of the last row.

2 ◆ Work a double crochet into this stitch in the usual way. Now continue back along the row, working a double crochet into each stitch. Instead of the usual chain effect along the edge, you will get a corded effect – crab stitch!

DOING A RUNNER

*Use this simple lacy runner to make a plain
table, sideboard or bookcase look special. The easy
pattern is made up of just treble stitch variations and chains and
it's trimmed with a crab stitch edging.*

SIZE

Finished runner measures
30cm (12in) × 90cm
(35½in).

YOU WILL NEED

2 × 50g (2oz) balls of Coats
Musica 8 crochet cotton

1.25mm crochet hook

ABBREVIATIONS
See page 9.

TENSION
40 sts and 18 rows to 10cm (4in)
measured over patt using 1.25mm
hook.

RUNNER
Main Section
Using 1.25mm hook, make 114 ch.
Foundation row (RS): 1 tr into 4th
ch from hook, 1 tr into each ch to
end, turn. 112 sts.
Now work in patt thus:
1st row: 3 ch (counts as 1 tr), 1 tr
into each of next 3 tr, *5 ch, (miss
2 tr, 1 dtr into next tr) 4 times, 5
ch, miss 2 tr, 1 tr into each of next

4 tr, rep from * to end, turn.
2nd row: 3 ch (counts as 1 tr), 1 tr
into each of next 3 tr, (5 ch, miss 5
ch, 1 dc into each of next 4 dtr, 5
ch, miss 5 ch, 1 tr into each of next
4 tr) to end, turn.
3rd row: 3 ch (counts as 1 tr), 1 tr
into each of next 3 tr, (5 ch, miss 5
ch, 1 dc into each of next 4 dc, 5
ch, miss 5 ch, 1 tr into each of next
4 tr) to end, turn.
4th row: as 3rd row.
5th row: 3 ch (counts as 1 tr), 1 tr
into each of next 3 tr, *2 ch, miss 5
ch, (1 dtr into next dc, 2 ch) 4
times, miss 5 ch, 1 tr into each of
next 4 tr, rep from * to end, turn.
6th row: 3 ch (counts as 1 tr), 1 tr
into each of next 3 tr, * (2 tr into
next ch sp, 1 tr into next dtr) 4
times, 2 tr into next ch sp, 1 tr into
each of next 4 tr, rep from * to
end, turn.
These 6 rows form patt and are
repeated.
Rep these 6 rows 25 times more,
but do *not* turn at end of last 6th
patt row.
Work Edging
1st round (RS): 1 ch (does *not*
count as st), 2 dc into each row
end to corner where foundation
ch begins, 3 dc into first ch of

foundation ch, 1 dc into each of
next 110 ch, 3 dc into next ch, 2 dc
into each row end edge to beg of
last row of Main Section, 3 dc into
first st of last row of Main Section,
1 dc into each of next 110 sts, 3 dc
into last st, ss to first dc.
2nd round: 4 ch (counts as 1 tr
and 1 ch), miss 2 dc, * (1 tr into
next dc, 1 ch, miss 1 ch) until tr
has been worked into central dc of
corner group of 3 dc, 4 ch (total of
5 ch now here), 1 tr into same
central dc of this corner group, 1
ch**, miss 2 dc, rep from * 3 times
more, ending last rep at **, miss 1
dc, ss to 3rd of 4 ch at beg of
round.
3rd round: 3 ch (counts as 1 tr), *
(1 tr into next ch sp, 1 tr into next
tr) to corner 5 ch sp, 1 tr into each
of next 2 ch, (2 tr, 1 dtr and 2 tr)
into next tr, 1 tr into each of next 2
ch, 1 tr into next tr, rep from * 3
times more, 1 tr into next ch sp, ss
to top of 3 ch at beg of round.
Now work one round of crab st (dc
worked from left to right, instead
of right to left) around entire
outer edge, ending with ss to
first st.
Fasten off.
Pin out to measurement; press.

FILET CROCHET

Filet crochet is a particular type of crochet in which
a mesh of solid and open blocks is made. The placement of these
solid blocks creates the design, and the pattern is followed
in a slightly different way to other crochet patterns.

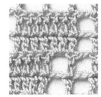

To understand filet crochet you need to think of the basic mesh as a grid of lines. You have a tall stitch (usually a treble) to form each of the vertical lines, and a string of chain stitches (usually two) to form the horizontal lines. The solid blocks are made by replacing the chain stitches that would run across the top of an open block with the same number of tall stitches, worked into the horizontal line below.

Most filet crochet patterns will start by giving you detailed instructions on how to set up your grid – the basic mesh. This will usually involve setting out the first few rows. At this point, you will know what type of tall stitch you work, and how many chain stitches there are across the top of each open block.

From here on, you follow a chart. Each square on the chart represents one block of the basic mesh – there will be a tall stitch at either side of the square and chain stitches at top and bottom. Each row of squares on the chart corresponds to a row of blocks on the crochet. Along with the chart will be instructions as to how to begin and end each row, and details of what to work to form an open or solid block. Once you have this information, you simply follow the chart, working the same basic mesh throughout and placing the open and solid blocks as they are on the chart. Blank squares on the chart represent open blocks, and filled ones solid blocks.

Shaping in filet crochet

Filet crochet is generally used to form rectangular panels, but sometimes there will be shaping along the side edges. This shaping is usually done by adding or subtracting complete blocks at the beginning or ends of rows. To decrease at the beginning of a row, slip stitch across the top of the last row worked until you reach the first vertical line needed for the next row. Now start this row in the usual way – but at the new point. To decrease at the end of a row, simply omit the required number of blocks and turn the work at this end point.

Sometimes the shaping is not quite as simple – you will be decreasing or increasing by forming half a block, either diagonally or widthwise. Take care to follow the pattern to see exactly how this decrease, or increase, is worked.

It is easiest and best to increase at the beginning of a row by making a new foundation chain for the new blocks.

Any increasing at ends of rows should be carefully explained in the pattern – the way this is worked will vary according to the type of basic mesh.

Circular filet crochet

It is also possible to make flat circles of filet crochet. As with most circular crochet work, you will start by working into a base ring. The first few rounds worked into this ring form the basis for the basic mesh. Once the basic mesh is established, the circle is formed by working lots of identical sections; think of them as being like slices of a cake. Between each 'slice' there will be stitches increased as the work progresses outwards.

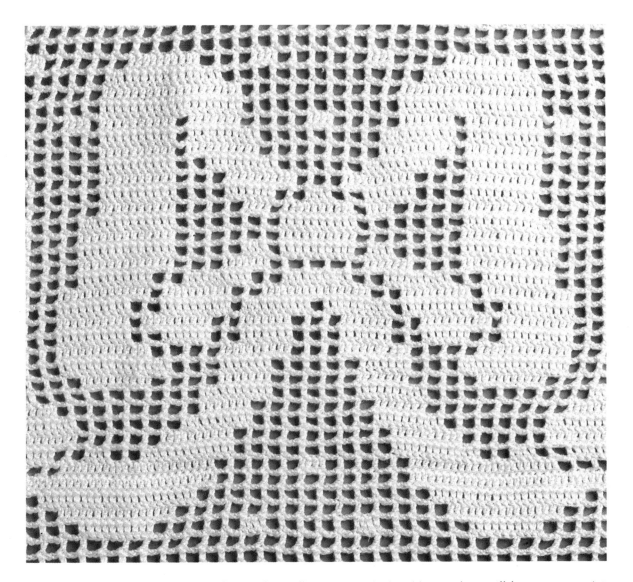

The chart for circular pieces of filet crochet will show only one of the sections, and the pattern will usually tell you how to work the increases between the sections. This section shown on the chart *must* be repeated as many times as the pattern says, otherwise your work will not lie flat.

Turning corners
Edgings of filet crochet are easy to make – they can be worked either lengthwise or widthwise.

If worked widthwise, there will be a corner point and the shaping worked into this corner point will be given in the pattern. Simply treat this type of filet crochet in the same way as you would any edging.

If an edging is worked lengthwise, the corners are usually mitred. To work the mitred corner, decreases of full blocks are made until you reach the outer corner point. For the second part of the corner, the row ends of the first part are used as the basis of the following rows.

TAKE A BOW

*A pretty bow design worked in rounds of filet mesh is echoed on
each of this tablecloth's six sections.*

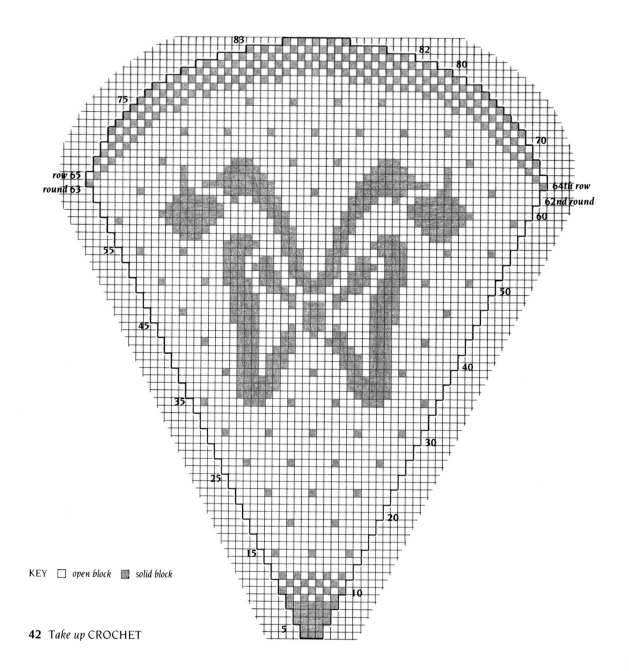

KEY ☐ *open block* ▨ *solid block*

SIZE

Finished cloth is 71cm (28in) in diameter at widest point.

YOU WILL NEED

3 × 50g (2oz) balls of Coats Musica 12 crochet cotton

1.00mm crochet hook

ABBREVIATIONS

See page 9.

TENSION

19 blocks and 23 rows to 10cm (4in) measured over filet mesh using 1.00mm hook.

NOTES

Chart shows one section – this is repeated 6 times, with either 3 ch or 5 ch separating each section. For basic filet mesh, work (2 ch, miss 2 sts, 1 tr into next tr) for open blocks, and (1 tr into each of next 3 sts) for solid blocks.

TABLECLOTH

Using 1.00mm hook, make 8 ch and join with ss to form a ring.

1st round: 3 ch (counts as 1 tr), 17 tr into ring, ss to top of 3 ch at beg of round.

2nd round: 5 ch (counts as 1 tr and 2 ch), (1 tr into next tr, 2 ch) 17 times, ss to 3rd of 5 ch at beg of round.

3rd round: 3 ch (counts as 1 tr), (2 tr into next sp, 1 tr into next tr), 17 times, 2 tr into last sp, ss to top of 3 ch at beg of round.

4th round: 6 ch (counts as 1 tr and 3 ch), 1 tr into base of 6 ch, * 1 tr into each of next 8 tr, (1 tr, 3 ch and 1 tr) into next tr, rep from * 4 times more, 1 tr into each of next 8 tr, ss to 3rd of 6 ch at beg of round, turn.

5th round: 3 ch (counts as 1 tr), 1 tr into each of next 9 tr, 5 ch, *miss 3 ch, 1 tr into each of next 10 tr, 5 ch, rep from * 4 times more, ss to top of 3 ch at beg of round, turn.

6th round: ss along to 3rd of 5 ch, 6 ch (counts as 1 tr and 3 ch), 1 tr into base of 6 ch, * 1 tr into each of next 2 ch, 1 tr into each of next 10 tr, 1 tr into each of next 2 ch, (1

tr, 3 ch and 1 tr) into next ch, rep from * 4 times more, 1 tr into each of next 2 ch, 1 tr into each of next 10 tr, 1 tr into each of next 2 ch, ss to 3rd of 6 ch at beg of round, turn.

These 6 rounds set filet mesh – there are now 6 sections of 5 solid blocks separated by 3 ch.

Cont to follow chart until 63rd round is complete, remembering to turn at end of each round.

Now work top of each section in rows by working rows 64–83 of chart.

Fasten off.

Pin out to measurement given and press.

BORDER LINES

*This filet crochet panel, depicting a flower bowl, has a
zig-zag filet crochet border that is worked in rounds. Use it as
here for the front panel of a fragrant cushion filled with
pot-pourri, or on its own as a table mat.*

SIZE

Finished centre panel
measures approx 35cm
(13¾in) × 24cm (9½in).
Edging is approx 8.5cm
(3¼in) at widest point.

YOU WILL NEED

2 × 50g balls of Coats
Virtuoso crochet cotton

1.50mm crochet hook

Cushion cover and pad
approx 35cm (13¾in) ×
24cm (9½in)

ABBREVIATIONS
See page 9.

TENSION
16 blocks and 18 rows to 10cm
(4in) measured over filet mesh
using 1.50mm hook.

CROCHET PANEL
Centre Section
Using 1.50mm hook, make 169 ch.
1st row (RS): 1 tr into 5th ch from
hook, 1 tr into each ch to end,
turn. 166 sts.

2nd row: 3 ch (counts as first tr),
1 tr into each of next 3 tr, (2 ch,
miss 2 tr, 1 tr into next tr) to last 3
sts, 1 tr into each of next 2 tr, 1 tr
into top of turning ch, turn. 55
blocks.
Last row forms basis of filet mesh.
Now work following chart, starting
with 3rd row.
Start each row with 3 ch (to count
as first tr) and end each row by
working into top of turning ch of
previous row.
Work open blocks as (2 ch, miss 2
sts, 1 tr into next tr) and solid
blocks as (1 tr into each of next 3
sts).
Cont as now set until all 43 rows
have been worked.
Do not fasten off or turn at end of
last row.
Edging
Now work around entire outer
edge of Centre Section as follows:
1st round (RS): 5 ch (counts as 1
tr and 2 ch), (1 dtr, 2 ch and 1 tr)
into base of first 5 ch – corner
point, work along row end edge as
follows: 3 tr around stem of tr at
end of 43rd row, (2 ch, miss
turning ch at beg of previous row,
4 tr around stem of tr at beg of
previous row) to next corner point

– base of last tr of first row of
Centre Section, (2 ch, 1 dtr, 2 ch
and 1 tr) into same corner point,
work along foundation ch edge as
follows: 1 tr into each of next 3 ch,
(2 ch, miss 2 ch, 1 tr into each of
next 4 ch) to next corner point –
base of turning ch at beg of first
row of Centre Section, (2 ch, 1 dtr,
2 ch and 1 tr) into same corner
point, work along next row end
edge as follows: 3 tr around
turning ch at beg of first row, (2
ch, miss tr at end of next row, 4 tr
around turning ch at beg of next
row) to next corner point – top of
turning ch at beg of 43rd row, (2
ch, 1 dtr, 2 ch and 1 tr) into same
corner point st, work across top of
43rd row thus: 1 tr into each of
next 3 tr, (2 ch, miss 2 tr, 1 tr into
each of next 3 tr) to end, omitting
1 tr at end of last rep, ss to 3rd of
5 ch at beg of round and along to
top of first dtr, turn.

2nd round: 5 ch (counts as 1 tr
and 2 ch), (1 dtr, 2 ch and 1 tr) into
top of dtr, *1 tr into each of next 3
sts, (2 ch, miss 2 sts, 1 tr into each
of next 4 sts) to next dtr, (2 ch, 1
dtr, 2 ch and 1 tr) into same dtr,
rep from * twice more, 1 tr into
each of next 3 sts, (2 ch, miss 2

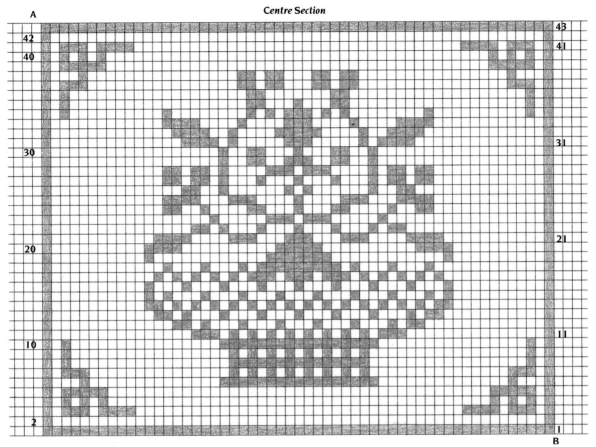

KEY   ☐ *open block*   ▨ *solid block*

sts, 1 tr into each of next 4 sts) to end, omitting last tr at end of last rep, ss to 3rd of 5 ch at beg of round and along to top of first dtr, turn.

These 2 rows form basis of filet mesh.

Now work chart given overleaf, starting with 3rd round and turning work at end of each round. Start each round with (5 ch – to count as 1 tr and 2 ch, (1 dtr, 2 ch and 1 tr) into same dtr) and end each round by working (ss into 3rd of 5 ch at beg of round and

along to top of first dtr, turn). Into other 3 corners – marked by a dtr – work (1 tr, 2 ch, 1 dtr, 2 ch and 1 tr).

Work open and solid blocks as for Centre Section.

Cont as now set until 8th round has been worked.

Now work 9th round but working solid corners as follows:

First corner: 3 ch (to count as 1 tr), (1 tr, 3 dtr and 2 tr) into same dtr.

Other corners: (2 tr, 3 dtr and 2 tr) into corner dtr.

Now work points of edging in rows as follows:

First Point

10th row: ss over next dtr and 2 tr, 3 ch (counts as 1 tr), 1 tr into each of next 6 sts, (2 ch, miss 2 sts, 1 tr into next tr) 3 times, 1 tr into each of next 3 sts, (2 ch, miss 2 sts, 1 tr into next st) 3 times, 1 tr into each of next 6 sts, turn. 11 blocks.

11th row: ss over last 3 tr of previous row and into next tr, 3 ch (counts as 1 tr), 1 tr into each of next 6 sts, (2 ch, miss 2 sts, 1 tr into next st) 5 times, 1 tr into each of next 6 sts, turn. 9 blocks.

12th row: ss over last 3 tr of previous row and into next tr, 3 ch (counts as 1 tr), 1 tr into each of next 6 sts, (2 ch, miss 2 sts, 1 tr

into next st) 3 times, 1 tr into each of next 6 sts, turn. 7 blocks.

13th row: ss over last 3 tr of previous row and into next tr, 3 ch (counts as 1 tr), 1 tr into each of next 6 sts, 2 ch, miss 2 sts, 1 tr

into each of next 7 sts, turn. 5 blocks.

14th row: ss over last 3 tr of previous row and into next tr, 3 ch (counts as 1 tr), 1 tr into each of next 9 sts, turn. 3 blocks.

Edging

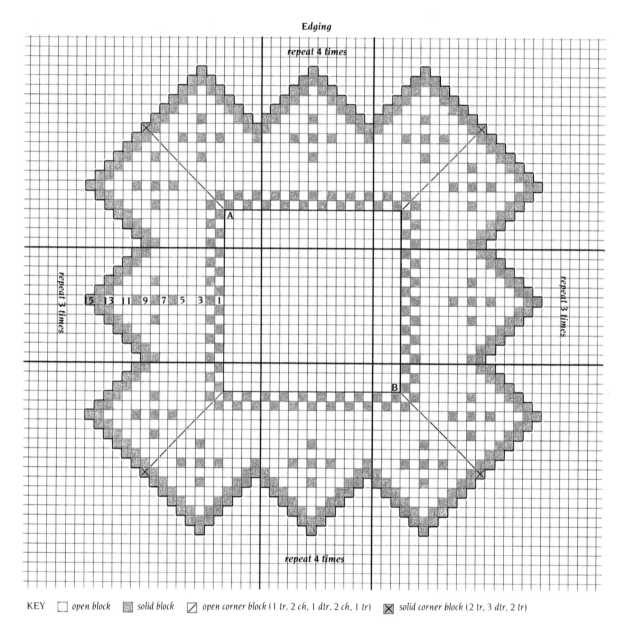

KEY   ☐ *open block*   ▨ *solid block*   ◩ *open corner block (1 tr, 2 ch, 1 dtr, 2 ch, 1 tr)*   ◪ *solid corner block (2 tr, 3 dtr, 2 tr)*

15th row: ss over last 3 tr of previous row and into next tr, 3 ch (counts as 1 tr), 1 tr into each of next 3 sts. 1 block.
Fasten off.

Second Point
Return to 9th round and attach yarn to 3rd st after last one used for First Point.
10th row: 3 ch (counts as 1 tr),

1 tr into each of next 6 sts, (2 ch, miss 2 sts, 1 tr into next tr) 7 times, 1 tr into each of next 6 sts, turn. 11 blocks.
Complete this point as for First Point by working 11th–15th rows.

All Remaining Points
Work as for Second Point, always rejoining yarn to 9th round 3 sts along from last st used for

previous point *except* at corners where yarn is rejoined on 6th st from last st used for previous point.

MAKING UP
Pin out to measurements given and press. Neatly hand sew panel to cushion front, with border extending beyond cushion edge.

COMING UP ROSES

*This delicate filet border, with its rose motifs
and its dainty scalloped edge, will add a touch of old-fashioned
charm to any setting. Worked lengthwise, it uses
a very fine crochet cotton.*

SIZE

Border is 11cm (4¼in) wide
at widest point. One full
repeat of border pattern
(39 rows) is 16cm (6¼in)
long.

YOU WILL NEED

2 × 50g (2oz) balls of Coats
Opera 30 crochet cotton

0.75mm crochet hook

Piece of fabric approx 50cm
(20in) × 35cm (14in) for
centre

ABBREVIATIONS
See page 9.
Special abbreviations: blk(s) –
block(s).

TENSION
22 blocks and 24 rows to 10cm
(4in) measured over filet mesh
pattern using 0.75mm hook.

Shaping Notes
SCALLOPED EDGE
Outer edge of border is scalloped.
This is formed by half block

increases and decreases. As chart
is an odd number of rows, shaping will not always appear at same
end of row as for previous repeat.
Work shaping as follows:
**Half block increase at beg of
row:** 6 ch (counts as 1 dtr and 2
ch), 1 tr into base of 6 ch, patt to
end, turn.
**Half block increase at end of
row:** patt to last st, 1 tr into last
st, 2 ch, 1 dtr into same place as
last tr, turn.
**Half block decrease at beg of
row:** 4 ch, miss first tr and next 2
sts, 1 tr into next st, patt to end,
turn.
**Half block decrease at end of
row:** patt to last 4 sts, yarn over
hook, insert hook into next st and
draw loop through, yarn over hook
and draw through 2 loops, (yarn
over hook) twice, miss 2 sts, insert
hook into next st – this is last st of
row – and draw loop through,
(yarn over hook and draw through
2 loops) twice, yarn over hook and
draw through all 3 loops on
hook, turn.

CORNERS
Corners of border are mitred.
Work starts at point of one corner

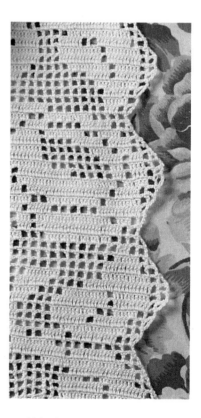

and blocks are then increased to
give full width of border. First
section of next corner is worked
by decreasing down to a point.
Second half of this corner is
worked by increasing out again to
full width. On this increased section, the row ends of the first

section are used as the 'foundation ch' of the increased sts.

BORDER

Using 0.75mm hook, make 14 ch.

1st row: 1 tr into 8th ch from hook (to form first open blk), 1 tr into each of next 3 ch (to form first solid blk), 2 ch, miss 2 ch, 1 tr into next ch (to form next open blk), 2 ch, 1 dtr into same place as last tr (to form increased half blk), turn.

2nd row: 5 ch (counts as 1 tr and 2 ch – first full open blk), miss (first dtr and 2 ch), 1 tr into next tr (forms 1 open blk), 1 tr into each of next 6 sts (forms 2 solid blks), 2 ch, miss 2 ch, 1 tr into next ch (forms one open blk), turn.

3rd row: 10 ch, 1 tr into 8th ch from hook, 2 ch, miss 2 ch, 1 tr into next tr (this is last tr of previous row – 2 blks increased), 2 ch, miss 2 ch, 1 tr into each of next 7 tr, 2 ch, miss 2 ch, (1 tr, 2 ch and 1 dtr) into next ch, turn.

4th row: 5 ch, miss (first dtr and 2 ch), 1 tr into each of next 13 sts, (2 ch, miss 2 ch, 1 tr into next st) twice, turn.

5th row: 10 ch, 1 tr into 8th ch from hook, (2 ch, miss 2 ch, 1 tr into next tr) twice, 1 tr into each of next 6 sts, 2 ch, miss 2 tr, 1 tr into each of next 7 sts, 2 ch, miss 2 ch, (1 tr, 2 ch and 1 dtr) into next ch, turn.

6th row: 5 ch, miss (first dtr and 2 ch), 1 tr into next tr, 2 ch, miss 2 ch, 1 tr into each of next 7 sts, 2 ch, miss 2 ch, 1 tr into each of next 13 sts, 2 ch, miss 2 ch, 1 tr into next ch, turn.

7th row: 10 ch, 1 tr into 8th ch

These 39 rows form one repeat

KEY
☐ open block
▨ solid block

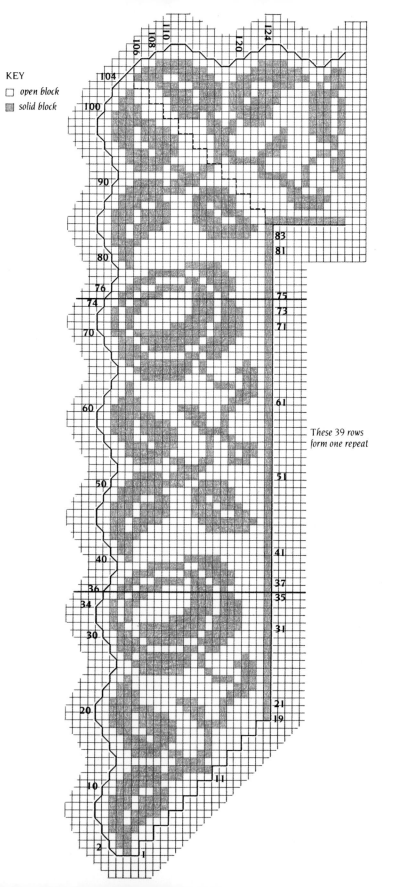

from hook, 2 ch, miss 2 ch, 1 tr into each of next 13 sts, 2 ch, miss 2 tr, 1 tr into each of next 10 sts, (2 ch, miss 2 ch, 1 tr into next st) twice, turn.

8th row: 4 ch (counts as 1 dtr – forms decreased half blk), miss (first tr and 2 ch), 1 tr into next tr, 2 ch, miss 2 ch, 1 tr into each of next 10 tr, 2 ch, miss 2 ch, 1 tr into each of next 13 tr, (2 ch, miss 2 ch, 1 tr into next st) twice, turn.

These 8 rows set filet mesh and start to shape first half of first corner.

Keeping filet mesh correct and working shaping as shown on chart and as detailed above, now cont following chart thus:

Complete rows 1 to 19 – first half of first corner completed.

*Work rows 20 to 74.

Now rep rows 36 to 74 once more, and then work rows 75 to 84.

Work rows 85 to 105, decreasing at inner edge as shown by line on chart – this forms first half of next corner.

Now work rows 106 to 124, using row ends of rows 85 to 105 as base ch.

Now work rows 20 to 105 again to form second side.

Complete this corner as for first by working rows 106 to 124.*

Rep from * to * to complete third and fourth sides.

Fasten off.

MAKING UP

Join corner seam. Pin out to measurement given and press. Trim and hem fabric to fit centre space of border, and then neatly hand stitch border to fabric.

Changing Yarn or Colour

Not many items can be made with just one
ball of yarn – so you need to know how to join in
new balls. Similarly, not everything you make will only use
one colour, and you need to know
how to change colours.

Adding new yarn

To keep the work neat and to avoid unsightly ends that may come loose, you should only join in new yarn at the edge of the work, if possible. Of course, this is rather difficult sometimes – especially with a circular piece, where there is no edge! Wherever you join in new yarn, do not tie a knot.

As the very last stage of any crochet stitch actually forms the first part of the next stitch, you therefore need to change colours of yarn just before you complete a stitch.

Normally the ends of yarn are dropped at the time of changing and are darned in later. But if you are working in a fairly solid stitch pattern, you can work over the loose ends, thereby avoiding the need to darn them in afterwards. The number of stitches worked over the ends will depend on the stitch pattern you are working and the thickness of the yarn.

If you are working **stripes**, strand the yarn loosely up the side of the work (or across the wrong side, if working in rounds) from stripe to stripe. Any edging can be worked over these loose strands, thereby fully enclosing them.

If you are working a design in two colours that contrast greatly, or which is very open and lacy, you may find that the colour not in use will actually show through from the right side – even if it is enclosed

with the stitches worked in the second colour. In these cases it is much better to use a separate ball of yarn for each block of colour, without stranding the yarn across the wrong side of the work or enclosing it in other stitches. When completed, darn in the loose ends, making sure that they are darned into the areas worked in the same colour.

Similarly, when joining edges where coloured sections meet, use the colour of yarn that matches the edges to be joined. This may involve using quite a few lengths of yarn to join the seam – but if you leave long ends, these can be used for the seam.

Following colourwork charts

Crochet designs in lots of colours are often worked following charts. On these charts each square of the chart represents one stitch, and one row of squares represents one row of stitches. Sometimes a chart will be shown in full colour but often charts are black and white, and symbols will appear within each square. These symbols signify the colour that is to be used for that stitch, and the key that accompanies the chart will explain which symbol relates to which colour of yarn. The written pattern will explain what stitch pattern you use as the basis for this chart and, from there on, you simply follow the chart, changing colour as you need to.

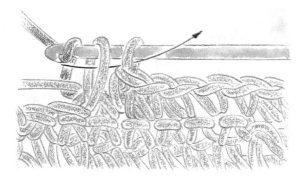

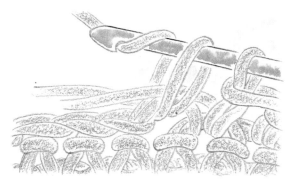

◆ If you need to join in new yarn across a row or round, simply drop the old yarn. Pick up the new yarn and complete the work. When you have finished, secure the two ends together firmly and darn in the loose ends.

◆ Alternatively, to work over loose ends, change to the new yarn and hold the two loose ends at the wrong side of the work. As you work the next few stitches, enclose these ends in with the new stitches. Once you are sure they will not come free, drop the ends and continue. Later on, you can snip off the free ends.

CHANGING COLOUR

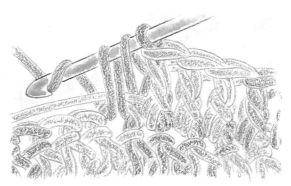

◆ Work the crochet until you have completed the stitch *before* the last one to be worked in that colour. Now work all but the very last 'yo and draw through' stage of the next stitch. Drop the old colour yarn and pick up the new colour. Complete the stitch using this new colour and continue working.

◆ There is no need to keep joining in and breaking off the yarn if there are lots of small areas to be worked in different colours. In the same way as you can work over the loose ends when joining in new yarn, you can carry a colour of yarn from one area to the next by simply enclosing the yarn in with the stitches between the two areas.

TEMPTING DESIGN

These unusual cushions are made using
just double crochet stitches! The colourful design is worked
from a chart and, as they use thick cotton yarn,
they are quick to make as well.

SIZE

Finished cushion is 40cm (16in) square.

YOU WILL NEED

5 × 50g (2oz) balls of Patons Laguna DK in main colour (M – cream or black)

1 × 50g (2oz) ball of same yarn in each of 4 contrast colours (A – light coral, B – brown, C – green and D – red)

3.50mm crochet hook

40cm (16in) square cushion pad

ABBREVIATIONS

See page 9.

TENSION

18 sts and 21 rows to 10cm (4in) measured over double crochet fabric using 3.50mm hook.

CUSHION BACK

Using 3.50mm hook and M, make 74 ch.

1st row (RS): 1 dc into 2nd ch from hook, 1 dc into each ch to end, turn. 73 sts.

2nd row: 1 ch (does *not* count as st), 1 dc into first dc, 1 dc into each dc to end, turn.

2nd row forms double crochet fabric and is repeated.

Work a further 82 rows.

Fasten off.

CUSHION FRONT

Work exactly as for Cushion Back, but following chart.

MAKING UP

Using B, embroider snake's tongue on cushion front. Sew front to back along 3 edges, insert cushion pad and close 4th edge.

KEY ☐ M (cream or black)   ▨ A (light coral)   ■ B (brown)   ☐ C (green)   ▨ D (red)

ADDING TEXTURE

*There are many ways of adding texture
to a crochet item – but they all use the same basic stitches.
It is the way these stitches are positioned
that creates the texture.*

Most crochet stitches are worked by inserting the hook, from front to back, under both of the chain loops across the top of the corresponding stitch one row below. By working the new stitch into a different place, texture is created. You can work into just one of the loops, at either the front or the back, or around the stem of the stitch, again from either the front or back.

Relief stitches

For a relief stitch, instead of working into the top of the stitch below, you work *around* the stem of it. The actual stitch is made in exactly the same way as usual, but into a different place.

Any stitch can be worked in this way – but, obviously, as you are working into a point below the top of the row the resulting stitch adds less height to the work. Similarly, if the base stitch is very short, there is virtually no stem to work around. The most common type of relief stitch is the relief treble, worked onto trebles or half trebles.

Working through one loop only

Instead of working through both of the loops that form the chain effect on the stitch below, texture can be added by working through just one loop. The resulting fabric has a line running across it, formed by the loops not picked up by the new stitches.

Stitch groups

Working lots of stitches into one place is not only used to create pretty patterns, it also adds surface interest. Groups of stitches can be joined at the top in different ways. A much more prominent bobble can be made with five trebles worked into one place by the way the separate stitches are joined at the top. To form a 'popcorn', or bell-type effect, work the trebles separately in the usual way. Now take the hook out of the last loop and insert it through the top of the first stitch of this group and back through the loop. Take the yarn over and round the hook and draw the loop through the loops on the hook. When you work back over this stitch group, you will only work into the one final stitch made – the others remain free and will form the open edge of the popcorn.

Textured motifs

Three-dimensional motifs can be made by working behind the stitches of a previous round, inserting the hook into or around the stitches of a round worked earlier. This method can be used to form rose-like flowers that can be centred in motifs or used as motifs on their own. Here, rounds are worked to form layers of petals, each new layer falling behind the previous one.

Once the first few rounds, which make up the inner top set of petals, are complete, make another round that goes to form the basis of the next round of petals by working behind these first petals. This will usually be a round of chain loops, secured to the back of the base round of the first set of petals. The next round of petals is then worked into these loops. You can continue in this way, building up layers of petals.

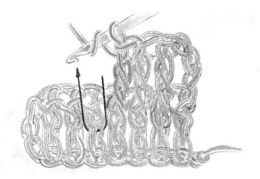

◆ To make a **relief front treble**, or '**rftr**', take the yarn over and round the hook and insert it through the work, from the front and from right to left, around the stem of the stitch below. Draw through a loop and complete the 'yo and draw through 2 loops' twice.

◆ To make a **relief back treble**, or '**rbtr**', the hook is inserted through the work, from the back and from right to left, round the stem of the stitch below.

LOOPS NOT PICKED UP

CLUSTERS

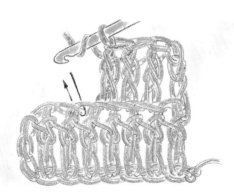

◆ Make this type of textured stitch in the way you normally would make the stitch, but, instead of inserting the hook under both loops, simply insert it under just one. The pattern will tell you whether you are to work through just the front or the back loop.

◆ Working five trebles together – a **tr5tog** – into one place will form a little bobble on the surface of the work. If these were worked into five different stitches, the effect would be much flatter, forming a fan shape. Working five trebles into the same place, but not joining them together at the top, will create a shell effect. Although this adds little surface texture, it creates a scalloped edge.

SET PIECES

*Use the same simple shell pattern made
up of treble stitch groups to create a pretty cheval set or a
bright breakfast setting. It's only the colours and the
edgings that change!*

SIZE

Small mat is 11cm (4¼in) square. Large mat is 30cm (12in) by 24cm (9⅜in).

YOU WILL NEED

Breakfast set

1 × 50g (2oz) ball of Coats Musica 5 crochet cotton in each of red and white

1.75mm crochet hook

Cheval set

2 × 50g (2oz) balls of Coats Musica 5 crochet cotton

1.75mm crochet hook

NOTES

Breakfast and Cheval Sets are made from same pattern, but Cheval Set is worked in one colour throughout. Breakfast Set consists of one small mat and one large mat. Cheval Set consists of two small mats and one large mat.

ABBREVIATIONS

See page 9.

TENSION

36 sts and 19 rows to 10cm (4in) measured over shell patt using 1.75mm hook.

Breakfast set

SMALL MAT (Make one)
Using 1.75mm hook and red, make 32 ch.
Foundation row (WS): 1 dc into 2nd ch from hook, *miss 2 ch, 5 tr into next ch, miss 2 ch, 1 dc into next ch, rep from * to end, turn. 31 sts.
Join in white and work in patt thus:
1st row (RS): using white, 3 ch (counts as first tr), 2 tr into dc at base of 3 ch, *miss 2 tr, 1 dc into next tr, miss 2 tr, 5 tr into next dc, rep from * to last 6 sts, miss 2 tr, 1 dc into next tr, miss 2 tr, 3 tr into next dc, turn.
2nd row: using red, 1 ch (does *not* count as st), 1 dc into first tr, *miss 2 tr, 5 tr into next dc, miss 2 tr, 1 dc into next tr, rep from * to end, turn.
These 2 rows form shell patt and are repeated.
Work a further 12 rows in patt as now set, thus ending after a 2nd

patt row using red. Turn at end of last row, do not break off yarns, and do not fasten off.
Work Edging
Now work edging around entire outer edge as follows:
1st round (RS): using red, 1 ch (does *not* count as st), 3 dc into first (corner) dc, (1 dc into each of next 9 sts, miss one st) twice, 1 dc into each of next 9 sts, 3 dc into last (corner) st, work 27 dc evenly along row end edge to next corner (omitting last and foundation rows, this is 3 dc for each tr or turning ch row end and 1 dc for each dc row end), now work along foundation ch edge as follows: 3 dc into first (corner) ch, (1 dc into each of next 9 ch, miss one ch) twice, 1 dc into each of next 9 ch, 3 dc into last (corner) ch, work 27 dc along remaining row end edge, ss to first dc.
*** Break off red.
2nd round: using white, 1 ch (does *not* count as st), 1 dc into each dc to end, working 3 dc into centre dc of corner group and ending with ss to first dc.**
Rep 2nd round twice more.
Fasten off.
Pin out and press.

LARGE MAT

Using 1.75mm hook and red, make 104 ch.

Work foundation row as for Small Mat. 103 sts.

Now work 40 rows in shell patt as for Small Mat, thus ending after a 2nd patt row using red. Turn at end of last row, do not break off yarns, and do not fasten off.

Work Edging

Now work edging around entire outer edge as follows:

1st round (RS): using red, 1 ch (does *not* count as st), 3 dc into first (corner) dc, (1 dc into each of next 33 sts, miss one st) twice, 1 dc into each of next 33 sts, 3 dc into last (corner) st, work 79 dc evenly along row end edge to next corner, now work along foundation ch edge as follows: 3 dc into first (corner) ch, (1 dc into each of next 33 ch, miss one ch) twice, 1 dc into each of next 33 ch, 3 dc into last (corner) ch, work 79 dc along remaining row end edge, ss to first dc.

Now complete as for Small Mat from * * *

Cheval set

(Make two Small Mats and one Large Mat)

Work all mats as for Breakfast Set to **, but using one colour throughout.

3rd round: ss to centre dc of corner group, 1 ch (does *not* count as st), 1 dc into this centre dc of corner, *miss 1 dc, 4 tr into next dc, miss 1 dc, 1 dc into next dc, rep from * to end, replacing last dc with ss to top of first dc. Fasten off.

LIGHT RELIEF

This rug will add a homely feel to a country kitchen.
It uses relief treble stitches to give the sculptured effect and,
as it is made in a machine washable cotton yarn, it's practical
as well. You could make another one in a pastel
colour for the bathroom or bedroom.

SIZE

Finished rug is approx 76cm (30in) wide and 117cm (46in) long excluding fringe.

YOU WILL NEED

22 × 50g (2oz) balls of Patons Laguna DK

3.00mm and 3.50mm crochet hooks

ABBREVIATIONS

See page 9.

Special abbreviations: rbhtr – relief back half treble worked thus: work half treble in usual way but inserting hook from back of work and from right to left around stem of stitch of previous row; **rbtr** – relief back treble worked thus: work treble in usual way but inserting hook from back of work and from right to left around stem of stitch of previous row; **rfhtr** – relief front half treble worked thus: work half treble in usual way but inserting hook from front of work and from right to left around stem of stitch of previous row; **rftr** – relief front treble worked thus: work treble in usual way but inserting hook from front of work and from right to left around stem of stitch of previous row.

TENSION

20 sts and 13 rows to 10cm (4in) measure over patt using 3.50mm hook.

DIAMOND PANEL (37 sts)

1st row (RS): 1 rbtr around each of next 37 sts.
2nd row: 1 rftr around each of next 37 sts.
Rep 1st and 2nd rows once more.
5th row: 1 rbtr around each of next 18 sts, 1 rftr around next st, 1 rbtr around each of next 18 sts.
6th row: 1 rftr around each of next 17 sts, 1 rbtr around each of next 3 sts, 1 rftr around each of next 17 sts.
7th row: 1 rbtr around each of next 16 sts, 1 rftr around each of next 5 sts, 1 rbtr around each of next 16 sts.
8th row: 1 rftr around each of next 15 sts, 1 rbtr around each of next 7 sts, 1 rftr around each of next 15 sts.
9th row: 1 rbtr around each of next 14 sts, 1 rftr around each of next 9 sts, 1 rbtr around each of next 14 sts.
10th row: 1 rftr around each of next 13 sts, 1 rbtr around each of next 11 sts, 1 rftr around each of next 13 sts.
11th row: 1 rbtr around each of next 12 sts, 1 rftr around each of next 13 sts, 1 rbtr around each of next 12 sts.
12th row: 1 rftr around each of next 11 sts, 1 rbtr around each of next 15 sts, 1 rftr around each of next 11 sts.
13th row: 1 rbtr around each of next 10 sts, 1 rftr around each of next 17 sts, 1 rbtr around each of next 10 sts.
14th row: 1 rftr around each of 10 sts, 1 rbtr around each of next 17 sts, 1 rftr around each of next 10 sts.
15th row: 1 rbtr around each of next 11 sts, 1 rftr around each of next 15 sts, 1 rbtr around each of next 11 sts.

16th row: 1 rftr around each of next 12 sts, 1 rbtr around each of next 13 sts, 1 rftr around each of next 12 sts.

17th row: 1 rbtr around each of next 13 sts, 1 rftr around each of next 11 sts, 1 rbtr around each of next 13 sts.

18th row: 1 rftr around each of next 14 sts, 1 rbtr around each of next 9 sts, 1 rftr around each of next 14 sts.

19th row: 1 rbtr around each of next 15 sts, 1 rftr around each of next 7 sts, 1 rbtr around each of next 15 sts.

20th row: 1 rftr around each of next 16 sts, 1 rbtr around each of next 5 sts, 1 rftr around each of next 16 sts.

21st row: 1 rbtr around each of next 17 sts, 1 rftr around each of next 3 sts, 1 rbtr around each of next 17 sts.

22nd row: 1 rftr around each of next 19 sts, 1 rbtr around next st, 1 rftr around each of next 19 sts.
Now rep 1st and 2nd rows twice more.
These 26 rows form diamond panel.

SQUARE PANEL (37 sts)
1st row (RS): 1 rbtr around each of next 37 sts.
2nd row: 1 rftr around each of next 37 sts.
Rep 1st and 2nd rows once more.
5th row: 1 rbtr around each of next 10 sts, 1 rftr around each of next 17 sts, 1 rbtr around each of next 10 sts.
6th row: 1 rftr around each of next 10 sts, 1 rbtr around each of next

17 sts, 1 rftr around each of next 10 sts.
Rep 5th and 6th rows 8 times more.
Now rep 1st and 2nd rows twice more.
These 26 rows form square panel.

RUG
Using 3.50mm hook, make 151 ch.
Foundation row (WS): 1 htr into 4th ch from hook, 1 htr into each ch to end, turn. 149 sts.
Commence rib
1st row (RS): 2 ch (counts as first st), *1 rftr around next st, 1 rbtr around next st, rep from * to last 2 sts, 1 rftr around next st, 1 rbhtr around turning ch, turn.
2nd row: 2 ch (counts as first st), *1 rbtr around next st, 1 rftr around next st, rep from * to last 2 sts, 1 rbtr around next st, 1 rfhtr around turning ch, turn.
These 2 rows form rib patt and are repeated.
Rep 1st and 2nd rows 3 times more.
Commence panels
9th row (RS): rib 10, work next 37 sts as first row of diamond panel, rib 9, work next 37 sts as first row of square panel, rib 9, work next 37 sts as first row of diamond panel, rib 10, turn.
10th row: rib 10, work next 37 sts as 2nd row of diamond panel, rib 9, work next 37 sts as 2nd row of square panel, rib 9, work next 37 sts as 2nd row of diamond panel, rib 10, turn.
Cont as now set until all 26 rows of panels are complete.
Now rep 1st and 2nd rows 4 times.

43rd row (RS): rib 10, work next 37 sts as first row of square panel, rib 9, work next 37 sts as first row of diamond panel, rib 9, work next 37 sts as first row of square panel, rib 10, turn.
44th row: rib 10, work next 37 sts as 2nd row of square panel, rib 9, work next 37 sts as 2nd row of diamond panel, rib 9, work next 37 sts as 2nd row of square panel, rib 10, turn.
Cont as now set until all 26 rows of panels are complete.
Now rep 1st and 2nd rows 4 times. 76 rows completed.
Now rep 9th – 76th rows again. 144 rows completed.
Do not fasten off.
Work Edging
Change to 3.00mm hook.
Edging row (RS): 1 ch (does not count as st), 1 dc into each st to last st, 3 dc into last st, change to 3.50mm hook and now work along row end edge, working 1 dc into each row end, do not turn, now work back along row end edge in crab st (dc worked from left to right, instead of right to left).
Fasten off.
Rejoin yarn to corner of foundation ch edge at end of completed side edging and, starting with 3.00mm hook, work edging row along remaining 2 edges as before.
Fasten off.
Fringe
Cut 20cm (8in) lengths of yarn and knot groups of 3 lengths of yarn through edge stitches of shorter ends and every following 4th stitch. Trim fringe ends level.

Well Cushioned

These stunning cushions use the easiest of textured stitches — by working the trebles around the stems of the previous stitches, clever effects are formed, such as radiating checks and diagonal stripes of texture.

SIZE

Circular cushion
Approx 35cm (14in) diameter.

Rectangular cushion
Approx 30cm (12in) by 40cm (16in).

YOU WILL NEED

Circular cushion

5 × 50g (2oz) balls of Patons Pearl DK

3.50mm crochet hook

35cm (14in) diameter cushion pad

Rectangular cushion

7 × 50g (2oz) balls of Patons Pearl DK

3.50mm crochet hook

30cm (12in) × 40cm (16in) cushion pad

ABBREVIATIONS

See page 9.

Special abbreviations: rbtr – relief back treble worked thus: work treble in usual way but inserting hook from back of work and from right to left around stem of stitch of previous row; **rftr** – relief front treble worked thus: work treble in usual way but inserting hook from front of work and from right to left around stem of stitch of previous row.

TENSION

Circular cushion 22 sts and 14 rows to 10cm (4in) measured over patt using 3.50mm hooks.
Rectangular cushion 22 sts and 14 rows to 10cm (4in) measured over patt using 3.50mm hook.

CIRCULAR CUSHION
First Side

Using 3.50mm hook, make 5 ch and join with a ss to form a ring.
1st round: 2 ch (counts as first st), 9 htr into ring, ss to top of 2 ch.
2nd round: 2 ch (counts as first st), 1 htr into each of next 9 sts, ss to top of 2 ch.
3rd round: 2 ch (counts as first st), 1 htr into st at base of 2 ch, (2 htr between st just worked and next st, 1 htr into next st) 9 times, 1 htr between st just worked and next st, ss to top of 2 ch.

4th round: 2 ch (counts as first st), 1 htr into each of next 29 sts, ss to top of 2 ch.
5th round: 2 ch (counts as first st), 1 htr into st at base of 2 ch, 1 htr into each of next 2 sts, *2 htr between st just worked and next st, 1 htr into each of next 3 sts, rep from * 8 times more, 1 htr between st just worked and next st, ss to top of 2 ch.
6th round: 2 ch (counts as first st), 1 htr into each of next 49 sts, ss to top of 2 ch.
7th round: 2 ch (counts as first st), 1 htr into st at base of 2 ch, 1 htr into each of next 4 sts, *2 htr between st just worked and next st, 1 htr into each of next 5 sts, rep from * 8 times more, 1 htr between st just worked and next st, ss to top of 2 ch.
8th round: 2 ch (counts as first st), 1 htr into each of next 69 sts, ss to top of 2 ch.
9th round: 2 ch (counts as first st), 1 rftr around st at base of 2 ch, 1 rbtr around each of next 5 sts, 1 rftr around next st, *2 htr between st just worked and next st, 1 rftr around next st, 1 rbtr around each of next 5 sts, 1 rftr around next st, rep from * 8 times more, 1 htr

between st just worked and next st, ss to top of 2 ch.

10th round: 2 ch (counts as first st), 1 rftr around next st, *1 rbtr around each of next 5 sts, 1 rftr around each of next 4 sts, rep from * 8 times more, 1 rbtr around each of next 5 sts, 1 rftr around each of next 2 sts, ss to top of 2 ch.

11th round: 2 ch (counts as first st), 1 rftr around st at base of 2 ch, 1 rftr around next st, 1 rbtr around each of next 5 sts, 1 rftr around each of next 2 sts, *2 htr between st just worked and next st, 1 rftr around each of next 2 sts, 1 rbtr around each of next 5 sts, 1 rftr around each of next 2 sts, rep from * 8 times more, 1 htr between st just worked and next st, ss to top of 2 ch.

12th round: 2 ch (counts as first st), 1 rftr around each of next 2 sts, *1 rbtr around each of next 5 sts, 1 rftr around each of next 6 sts, rep from * 8 times more, 1 rbtr around each of next 5 sts, 1 rftr around each of next 3 sts, ss to top of 2 ch.

13th round: 2 ch (counts as first st), 1 rbtr around st at base of 2 ch, 1 rbtr around each of next 2 sts, 1 rftr around each of next 5 sts, 1 rbtr around each of next 3 sts, *2 htr between st just worked and next st, 1 rbtr around each of next 3 sts, 1 rftr around each of next 5 sts, 1 rbtr around each of next 3 sts, rep from * 8 times more, 1 htr between st just worked and next st, ss to top of 2 ch.

14th round: 2 ch (counts as first st), 1 rbtr around each of next 3

sts, *1 rftr around each of next 5 sts, 1 rbtr around each of next 8 sts, rep from * 8 times more, 1 rftr around each of next 5 sts, 1 rbtr around each of next 4 sts, ss to top of 2 ch.

15th round: 2 ch (counts as first st), 1 rbtr around st at base of 2 ch, 1 rbtr around each of next 3 sts, 1 rftr around each of next 5 sts, 1 rbtr around each of next 4 sts, *2 htr between st just worked and next st, 1 rbtr around each of next 4 sts, 1 rftr around each of next 5 sts, 1 rbtr around each of next 4 sts, rep from * 8 times more, 1 htr between st just worked and next st, ss to top of 2 ch.

16th round: 2 ch (counts as first st), 1 rbtr around each of next 4 sts, *1 rftr around each of next 5 sts, 1 rbtr around each of next 10 sts, rep from * 8 times more, 1 rftr around each of next 5 sts, 1 rbtr around each of next 5 sts, ss to top of 2 ch.

17th round: 2 ch (counts as first st), 1 rftr around st at base of 2 ch, 1 rftr around each of next 4 sts, 1 rbtr around each of next 5 sts, 1 rftr around each of next 5 sts, *2 htr between st just worked and next st, 1 rftr around each of next 5 sts, 1 rbtr around each of next 5 sts, 1 rftr around each of next 5 sts, rep from * 8 times more, 1 htr between st just worked and next st, ss to top of 2 ch.

18th round: 2 ch (counts as first st), *1 rftr around each of next 5 sts, 1 rbtr around each of next 5 sts, 1 rftr around each of next 5 sts, 1 rbtr around each of next 2 sts, rep from * 8 times more, 1 rftr

around each of next 5 sts, 1 rbtr around each of next 5 sts, 1 rftr around each of next 5 sts, 1 rbtr around next st, ss to top of 2 ch.

19th round: 2 ch (counts as first st), 1 rbtr around st at base of 2 ch, 1 rftr around each of next 5 sts, 1 rbtr around each of next 5 sts, 1 rftr around each of next 5 sts, 1 rbtr around next st, *2 htr between st just worked and next st, 1 rbtr around next st, 1 rftr around each of next 5 sts, 1 rbtr around each of next 5 sts, 1 rftr around each of next 5 sts, 1 rbtr around next st, rep from * 8 times more, 1 htr between st just worked and next st, ss to top of 2 ch.

20th round: 2 ch (counts as first st), 1 rbtr around next st, *1 rftr around each of next 5 sts, 1 rbtr around each of next 5 sts, 1 rftr around each of next 5 sts, 1 rbtr around each of next 4 sts, rep from * 8 times more, 1 rftr around each of next 5 sts, 1 rbtr around each of next 5 sts, 1 rftr around each of next 5 sts, 1 rbtr around each of next 2 sts, ss to top of 2 ch.

21st round: 2 ch (counts as first st), 1 rftr around st at base of 2 ch, 1 rftr around next st, 1 rbtr around each of next 5 sts, 1 rftr around each of next 5 sts, 1 rbtr around each of next 5 sts, 1 rftr around each of next 2 sts, *2 htr between st just worked and next st, 1 rftr around each of next 2 sts, 1 rbtr around each of next 5 sts, 1 rftr around each of next 5 sts, 1 rbtr around each of next 5 sts, 1 rftr around each of next 2 sts, rep from * 8 times more, 1 htr

between st just worked and next st, ss to top of 2 ch.

22nd round: 2 ch (counts as first st), 1 rftr around each of next 2 sts, *1 rbtr around each of next 5 sts, 1 rftr around each of next 5 sts, 1 rbtr around each of next 5 sts, 1 rftr around each of next 6 sts, rep from * 8 times more, 1 rbtr around each of next 5 sts, 1 rftr around each of next 5 sts, 1 rbtr around each of next 5 sts, 1 rftr around each of next 3 sts, ss to top of 2 ch.

23rd round: 2 ch (counts as first st), 1 rftr around st at base of 2 ch, 1 rftr around each of next 2 sts, 1 rbtr around each of next 5 sts, 1 rftr around each of next 5 sts, 1 rbtr around each of next 5 sts, 1 rftr around each of next 3 sts, *2 htr between st just worked and next st, 1 rftr around each of next 3 sts, 1 rbtr around each of next 5 sts, 1 rftr around each of next 5 sts, 1 rbtr around each of next 5 sts, 1 rftr around each of next 3 sts, rep from * 8 times more, 1 htr between st just worked and next st, ss to top of 2 ch.

24th round: 2 ch (counts as first st), 1 rftr around each of next 3 sts, *1 rbtr around each of next 5 sts, 1 rftr around each of next 5 sts, 1 rbtr around each of next 5 sts, 1 rftr around each of next 8 sts, rep from * 8 times more, 1 rbtr around each of next 5 sts, 1 rftr around each of next 5 sts, 1 rbtr around each of next 5 sts, 1 rftr around each of next 4 sts, ss to top of 2 ch. Fasten off.

Second Side

Work exactly as for First Side, but do not fasten off.

Holding sides WS facing, work one round of dc through last round of both sides to join edges, inserting cushion pad when seam is half complete.

Now work one round of crab st (dc worked from left to right, instead of right to left) around edge. Fasten off.

RECTANGULAR CUSHION

Using 3.50mm hook, make 132 ch and join with a ss to form a ring, taking care not to twist ch.

Foundation round: 2 ch (counts as first st), 1 htr into each ch to end, ss to top of 2 ch. 132 sts.

Now work in diagonal patt thus:

1st round (RS): 2 ch (counts as first st), 1 rftr around each of next 5 sts, *1 rbtr around each of next 6 sts, 1 rftr around each of next 6 sts, rep from * to last 6 sts, 1 rbtr around each of next 6 sts, ss to top of 2 ch.

2nd round: 2 ch (counts as first st), 1 rftr around each of next 4 sts, *1 rbtr around each of next 6 sts, 1 rftr around each of next 6 sts, rep from * to last 7 sts, 1 rbtr

around each of next 6 sts, 1 rftr
around next st, ss to top of 2 ch.
3rd round: 2 ch (counts as first
st), 1 rftr around each of next 3
sts, *1 rbtr around each of next 6
sts, 1 rftr around each of next 6
sts, rep from * to last 8 sts, 1 rbtr
around each of next 6 sts, 1 rftr
around each of next 2 sts, ss to
top of 2 ch.
4th round: 2 ch (counts as first
st), 1 rftr around each of next 2
sts, *1 rbtr around each of next 6
sts, 1 rftr around each of next 6
sts, rep from * to last 9 sts, 1 rbtr
around each of next 6 sts, 1 rftr
around each of next 3 sts, ss to
top of 2 ch.
5th round: 2 ch (counts as first
st), 1 rftr around next st, *1 rbtr
around each of next 6 sts, 1 rftr
around each of next 6 sts, rep
from * to last 10 sts, 1 rbtr around
each of next 6 sts, 1 rftr around
each of next 4 sts, ss to top of 2
ch.
6th round: 2 ch (counts as first
st), *1 rbtr around each of next 6
sts, 1 rftr around each of next 6
sts, rep from * to last 11 sts, 1 rbtr

around each of next 6 sts, 1 rftr
around each of next 5 sts, ss to
top of 2 ch.
7th round: 2 ch (counts as first
st), 1 rbtr around each of next 5
sts, *1 rftr around each of next 6
sts, 1 rbtr around each of next 6
sts, rep from * to last 6 sts, 1 rftr
around each of next 6 sts, ss to
top of 2 ch.
8th round: 2 ch (counts as first
st), 1 rbtr around each of next 4
sts, *1 rftr around each of next 6
sts, 1 rbtr around each of next 6
sts, rep from * to last 7 sts, 1 rftr
around each of next 6 sts, 1 rbtr
around next st, ss to top of 2 ch.
9th round: 2 ch (counts as first
st), 1 rbtr around each of next 3
sts, *1 rftr around each of next 6
sts, 1 rbtr around each of next 6
sts, rep from * to last 8 sts, 1 rftr
around each of next 6 sts, 1 rbtr
around each of next 2 sts, ss to
top of 2 ch.
10th round: 2 ch (counts as first
st), 1 rbtr around each of next 2
sts, *1 rftr around each of next 6
sts, 1 rbtr around each of next 6
sts, rep from * to last 9 sts, 1 rftr

around each of next 6 sts, 1 rbtr
around each of next 3 sts, ss to
top of 2 ch.
11th round: 2 ch (counts as first
st), 1 rbtr around next st, *1 rftr
around each of next 6 sts, 1 rbtr
around each of next 6 sts, rep
from * to last 10 sts, 1 rftr
around each of next 6 sts, 1 rbtr
around each of next 4 sts, ss to
top of 2 ch.
12th round: 2 ch (counts as first
st), *1 rftr around each of next 6
sts, 1 rbtr around each of next 6
sts, rep from * to last 11 sts, 1 rftr
around each of next 6 sts, 1 rbtr
around each of next 5 sts, ss to
top of 2 ch.
These 12 rounds form diagonal
patt and are repeated.
Rep last 12 rounds 3 times more,
and then 1st – 6th rounds again.
Fasten off.
Fold tube in half and close one
end by working one row of dc
through both layers. Now work one
row of crab st (dc worked from left
to right) along this edge. Fasten
off. Insert cushion pad and close
remaining edge in same way.

MAKING UP

Once you have finished crocheting the pieces that make up an
item, they need to be joined correctly.

The way in which seams are joined can vary – they can be hand sewn together or joined with a row of crochet stitches. If pieces are to be joined by **hand sewing** use the same yarn as was used for the crocheted sections. If a long end is left, either at the beginning or end of the work, this end can be used for the sewing up. Use a large-eyed blunt needle so the strands that make up the yarn are gently pushed apart, rather than being split and weakened.

Joining seams by crocheting is quick and easy, and because it is just as flexible as the main crochet work it will not distort the finished item. Use the same size hook as was used for the main pieces and, obviously, the same yarn. When joining row-end edges, insert the hook through both layers of fabric in the same way as you would if you were working a crochet edging. Once all the seams are joined, darn in any remaining loose ends.

JOINING SEAMS

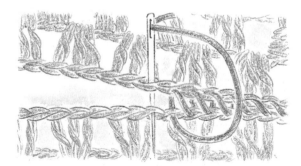

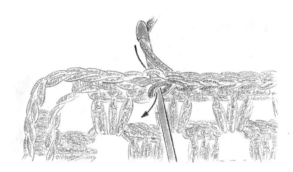

◆ When hand sewing crochet seams, the stitch you use to join the seam will depend on the type of crochet stitch pattern used. For seams where you are joining two row-top edges, you can use backstitch, working each stitch under both the loops of the stitches forming the row-top edges. This will, however, create quite a bulky seam. To form a much flatter seam, join the edges with small overcast stitches.

◆ To join two row-top edges together by crocheting, hold the two sections with right sides facing. Attach the yarn at one end of the seam and work one row of double crochet along the edge. Across the top of the seam, before it is joined, there are two rows of loops forming the chain effect. Work each crochet seam stitch taking just one loop from each edge, and work one seam stitch for each stitch along the edge.

FLOWER POWER

This little mat is an ideal way to use up leftover balls of coloured crochet cotton! Try making the flowers all in one colour as here, or use lots of different shades.

SIZE

Finished mat is approx 21cm (8¼ in) in diameter.

YOU WILL NEED

1 × 50g (2oz) ball of Coats Virtuoso crochet cotton in each of three colours (M – cream, A – pink and B – green)

1.50mm crochet hook

ABBREVIATIONS
See page 9.

TENSION
One flower measures 4cm (1½ in) in diameter using 1.50mm hook.

FLOWER (Make 6)
Using 1.50mm hook and A, make 5 ch and join with a ss to form a ring.
1st round: 5 ch (counts as 1 tr and 2 ch), (1 tr into ring, 2 ch) 7 times, ss to 3rd of 5 ch at beg of round.
2nd round: (1 dc, 1ch, 2 tr, 1 ch and 1 dc) into each ch sp to end.
3rd round: working behind petals formed by 2nd round, proceed as follows: 1 dc around stem of tr of 1st round between first and last petals of 2nd round, 3 ch, (1 dc around stem of next tr of 1st round, 3 ch) 7 times, ss to first dc.
4th round: 4 ch (counts as 1 dtr), (1 tr, 1 ch, 1 dc, 1 ch, 1 tr and 1 dtr) into first ch sp, (1 dtr, 1 tr, 1 ch, 1 dc, 1 ch, 1 tr and 1 dtr) into each ch sp to end, ss to top of 4 ch at beg of round.
5th round: 1 ch, working behind petals of 4th round, proceed as follows: (1 tr around dc of 3rd round, 3 ch) 8 times, ss to first tr.
6th round: (1 dc, 1 ch, 1 tr, 3 dtr, 1 tr, 1 ch and 1 dc) into each ch sp to end.
Fasten off.
Make another 5 flowers in the same way.

LEAVES (Make 12 in total)
First Leaf
Using 1.50mm hook and B, make 11 ch.
1st row: 1 dc into 2nd ch from hook, 1 dc into each of next 8 ch, 3 dc into last ch, now working back along strip into remaining loop of foundation ch, proceed as follows: 1 dc into each of next 7 ch, turn.

Now proceed as follows, *working into back loops of sts only:*
2nd row: 1 ch, 1 dc into first dc, 1 dc into each of next 7 dc, 3 dc into next dc, 1 dc into each of next 7 dc, turn.
3rd row: ss to central dtr of one petal of one Flower, 1 dc into first dc of Leaf, 1 dc into each of next 7 dc, 3 dc into next dc, 1 dc into each of next 7 dc, turn.
4th row: as 2nd row.
5th row: as 2nd row.
6th row: as 2nd row.
7th row: ss to central dtr of next petal of same Flower, 1 dc into first dc of Leaf, 1 dc into each of next 7 dc, ss to next dc.
Fasten off.
Second Leaf
Work as for first Leaf to end of 1st row.
2nd row: ss to central dtr of one petal of second Flower, 1 dc into first dc of Leaf, 1 dc into each of next 7 dc, 3 dc into next dc, 1 dc into each of next 7 dc, turn.
3rd row: 1 ch, 1 dc into first dc, 1 dc into each of next 7 dc, 3 dc into next dc, 1 dc into each of next 7 dc, turn.
4th row: as 3rd row.
5th row: as 3rd row.
6th row: as 2nd row.

7th row: I tr into ch sp at beg of 6th row of first Leaf, I dc into first dc of second Leaf, I dc into each of next 7 dc, ss to next dc. Fasten off.

Third Leaf
Work as for first Leaf, joining it to second Flower, leaving two petals free between Leaves.

Fourth Leaf
Work as for second Leaf, joining it to third Flower and third Leaf.

Fifth Leaf
Work as for first Leaf, joining it to third Flower, leaving two petals free between Leaves.

Sixth Leaf
Work as for second Leaf, joining it to fourth Flower and fifth Leaf. Cont in this way, making and joining Leaves to each other and Flowers, until 11 Leaves are complete.

Twelfth Leaf
Work as for second Leaf, joining it to remaining edge of first Flower and eleventh Leaf and taking care not to twist strip when joining Leaves.

Joined Leaves and Flowers now form a ring – along inner edge there are two free petals on each Flower between Leaves, and base points of Leaves (the point where yarn was fastened off) are free.

CENTRE SECTION
Using 1.50mm hook and M, make 10 ch and join with a ss to form a ring.

1st round: 5 ch (counts as I dtr and I ch), (I dtr into ring, I ch) 23 times, ss to 4th of 5ch at beg of round.

2nd round: 6 ch (counts as I dtr

and 2 ch), (miss I ch, I dtr into next dtr, 2 ch) 23 times, ss to 4th of 6 ch at beg of round.

3rd round: 11 ch (counts as I dtr and 7 ch), *miss (2 ch, I dtr and 2 ch), I dtr into next dtr, 7 ch, rep from * 10 times more, ss to 4th of 11 ch at beg of round.

4th round: 6 ch (counts as I dtr and 2 ch), 4 tr into next ch sp, 2 ch, (I dtr into next dtr, 2 ch, 4 tr into next ch sp, 2 ch) 11 times, ss to 4th of 6 ch at beg of round.

5th round: 6 ch (counts as I dtr and 2 ch), I dtr into base of 6 ch, 3 ch, miss 2 ch, I tr into each of next 4 tr, 3 ch, *miss 2 ch, (I dtr, 2 ch and I dtr) into next dtr, 3 ch, miss 2 ch, I tr into each of next 4 tr, 3 ch, rep from * 10 times more, ss to 4th of 6 ch at beg of round.

6th round: 4 ch (counts as I dtr), 4 dtr into first ch sp, 5 ch, miss (1

dtr, 3 ch and I tr), I tr into each of next 2 tr, 5 ch, *miss (I tr, 3 ch and I dtr), 5 dtr into next ch sp, 5 ch, miss (I dtr, 3 ch and I tr), I tr into each of next 2 tr, 5 ch, rep from * 10 times more, ss to top of 4 ch at beg of round.

7th round: I ch (counts as first dc), I dc into each of next 4 dtr, 5 ch, miss 5 ch, I dtr between next 2 tr, 5 ch, *miss 5 ch, I dc into each of next 5 dtr, 5 ch, miss 5 ch, I dtr between next 2 tr, 5 ch, rep from * 10 times more, ss to first dc.

8th round: I ch (counts as first dc), I dc into each st to end, ss to first dc.

9th round: 4 ch (counts as I tr and I ch), miss first 2 sts, (I tr into next dc, I ch, miss I dc) to end, ss to 3rd of 4 ch at beg of round.

Join Flowers and Leaves to Centre Section

10th round: ss into first ch sp, I ch (does *not* count as st), I dc into same ch sp, *3 ch, I dc into second free petal of one Flower, 6 ch, miss 3 ch sps of Centre Section, I dc into next ch sp, 6 ch, I dc into base point of next Leaf, 3 ch, miss 3 ch sps of Centre Section, I dc into next ch sp, 3 ch, I dc into base point of next Leaf, 6 ch, miss 3 ch sps of Centre Section, I dc into next ch sp, 6 ch, I dc into first free petal of next Flower, 3 ch, miss 3 ch sps of Centre Section **, I dc into next ch sp, rep from * 5 times more, ending last rep at **, ss to top of first dc.

Fasten off.

Pin out to measurement given and press, taking care not to squash flower petals.

INDEX

ACKNOWLEDGEMENTS

All crochet and hand-knitting yarns used for the items in
this book were kindly supplied by Coats Patons Crafts. For
details of your local stockist, contact: Consumer Services,
Coats Patons Crafts, P O Box 22, Darlington, Co. Durham
DL1 1YQ.
    Many thanks to Debbie Scott and Caroline Ashman for
their support and help, and to Pat Rhodes, Mrs Lawford and
Jenny Chapman for the many hours they spent crocheting!